Entertaining
for all seasons

Food display on page 36 by Ruth Ehrhardt

Paintings on pages 9, 15, 18, 20, 26, 27, 42, 51, 58, 62, 63, 73 by Julia Semokaitis

Paintings on pages 12, 19, 22 by Stanley Semokaitis

Painting on page 19 by Kapaka Senko

First published in the United States of America by Pink Peppercorn Press™, Oxnard, CA.

Library of Congress Cataloging-in-Publication Data is available by request.

Library of Congress Control Number: 2009938440

ISBN 978-0-578-03626-7

Copyright © 2009 by Kapaka L. Senko

All rights reserved. No part of this book may be reproduced or transmitted in any form by any means, electronic or mechanical, including photocopying and recording, or by any information storage or retrieval system, except as may be expressly permitted, without prior permission in writing from the publisher.

Requests for such permissions should be addressed to:

Pink Peppercorn Press™
627 Transom Way
Oxnard, CA 93035

Distributed by Lulu.com

Acknowledgment:

My editor's good judgment and unfailing support made our collaborations intensely creative fun! Thanks go to my loving, generous family who always appreciates and encourages my creative productions.

Entertaining
for all seasons

Kapaka L. Senko

Let's follow the sun on fairy wings,
Alight now and then in foreign places,
To sip and sup and speak of homey things,

Drink glögg in Denmark on Christmas Day,
And Irish coffee on St. Patty's Night,
Champagne in Paris at a spring soiree,

Eat summer berries on the Seine,
Hot dogs with mustard on the 4th of July,
And tapas this fall in sunny Spain,

On fairy wings, let's follow the year,
We'll celebrate the days of our lives,
If only at home--for family's there.

Content

8 Winter's Coming

Signs of Christmas
Christmas Trees
Company Holiday Party
Christmas Dinner Traditions
Christmas Decorating
New Year's Eve
New Year's Day
Winter Wonderland
Winter Blooms

Martin Luther King Day
Chinese New Year
Valentine's Day
Valentine Party
President's Day
American Country
St. Patrick's Day
Irish Flair

26 Spring Time

Fresh Start
April in Paris
A Parisian Soiree
Easter
Easter Traditions
Outdoor Decorating
Cinco de Mayo
Mother's Day
Mother's Day Brunch

Memorial Day
Celebrating Heroes
Graduation Celebrations
"Staycation"
Father's Day
Celebrating Dad

42 Summer Fun

Garden Party
Summer's Day
Extend Indoor Comfort
4th of July
4th of July Barbecue
4th of July Pageant
Kids Entertain
Midsummer Romance
Card Readings

Create Outdoors
Build a Playhouse
Indian Dining
Spice Land
Labor Day
Hawaiian Islands Backyard
Seashore Get-Away
Bateaux Mouches

60 Autumn Displays

Bay Window Vignette
Autumn Indoors
Conversational Groupings
Halloween Festivities
Pumpkin Carving Party
Halloween
Trick or Treat
Veteran's Day

Tapas Party
Wine Tasting
Italian Dinner Finale
Thanksgiving
Thanksgiving Banquet
Thanksgiving Choices
Thanksgiving Buffet

Content

Menus

- 11 Christmas Get-Together
- 14 Russian Dinner
- 15 Finger Food
- 18 Splendors of Africa
- 19 Chinese Banquet
- 20 Breakfast in Bed
- 21 Afternoon Tea
- 23 Down Home Fare
- 25 Irish Feast
- 27 Spring Dinner Party
- 29 French Buffet
- 33 Fiesta Party
- 35 Make-ahead Mom's Meal
- 36 Make-ahead Meal (Memorial Day)
- 38 Open House
- 39 Cuban Fare
- 41 Barbecue for Dad
- 43 Garden Party
- 47 July 4th Barbecue
- 50 Moroccan Feast
- 55 Indian Sampler
- 56 Luau
- 59 Supper on the Seine
- 65 Oktoberfest
- 71 Multo Bene Mangi
- 72 Simple Supper

Favorite Recipes

- 11 Sun-dried Tomato Spirals
- 19 Peking Pancakes
- 23 Rachel's Cherry Cream Cheese Pie
- 23 Yam Bams (Biscuits)
- 25 Annie's Famous Irish Soda Bread
- 29 Salade avec Chêvre
- 31 Giant Yellow Easter Egg
- 35 Fancy Potato Salad
- 41 George's Black Forest Cake
- 47 July 5th Corn Salad
- 56 Easy Exotic Ribs
- 59 Coquilles St. Jacques
- 65 Harvest Muffins
- 67 Gobblin' Good Sweet Potato
- 68 Navy Bean Soup

Tips

- 9   Gifts for Children to Make
- 10 Creating Tree Magic
- 14 Create Drama
- 15 Service Table Tips
- 16 Winter Decorating
- 17 Amaryllis Care
- 21 Valentine Party Ideas
- 24 Ethnic Parties
- 32 Create Garden Rooms
- 32 Decorate Your Garden
- 38 Honoree Table
- 40 Theme Parties for Dad
- 41 Craft a Photo Album
- 43 Tablecloth Transformation
- 46 Showcasing Fabrics
- 48 Pageant Creation
- 52 Create Garden Magic
- 55 Indian Culinary Terms
- 59 Form a Gourmet Dinner Club
- 64 Halloween Entertainment
- 65 Pumpkin Carving Techniques
- 68 Creating a Tribute
- 72 At Home Entertainment
- 73 Food Presentation Tips
- 75 Set Up Serving Stations

Etcetera

- 2   Acknowledgements
- 6   Introduction
- 77 Afterword
- 78 Index

Introduction

Dear Reader, welcome to my eclectic home, really an adult-size playhouse. Here, I stage "events" to my heart's content! Changing seasons and intriguing international cuisines inspire my productions inside and out. You're invited to a behind the scenes look at my entertaining events over the span of a year. I want to encourage you to take your homemaking arts to a new level of exuberance! Why? It's a way to make life more amusing and fulfilling for you and those you love.

The fun part of entertaining for me is a bit of grown-up make believe. Think of entertaining as putting on a theatrical production. With a script for fun in mind, become set designer, director, producer, even a star in your own show. Include your family and guests as cast, crew, and audience. Invite them to come in costume!

What if every holiday were like a visit to a different land in the Magic Kingdom? If travel is not an option, it is still possible to "vacation" at home in ways your family and friends will enjoy and remember for a lifetime.

There is no right way to decorate a home or create a wonderland experience. It has to look and feel right to you. No matter what your style choice is or budget limitations, you can add seasonal decorations and international flavor to enhance it. Your innate preference for simplicity, judicious collection, or riotous clutter will shine through. Certain cuisines will call to you. Be sure to answer! Novel activities may come to mind. Original ideas are good! Try them out! Give yourself permission to unleash the unique, passionate hostess (and theatrical producer) from within.

Animate *your thinking. Use your home as an ever-changing canvas for creative self-expression. Engage young and old in your sense of beauty, fun, and adventure. It's liberating to experience uninhibited playfulness. Where you lead, children will follow.*

Inside this Book
Celebrating 4 seasons, 17 holidays

Money-saving tips for decorating

Display guidelines

Entertaining ideas

Craft instructions

Menu suggestions and recipes

Personal anecdotes

Music and movie recommendations

International theme parties

Home and garden tips

Creative Self-Expression

Winter's Coming

Can't Wait for Christmas?

The day after Thanksgiving is officially Christmas season kick-off at our house, however tempting it is to put up decorations earlier!

This year, I just couldn't wait! I put up a small, pre-lit tree with glass pine cone ornaments. To this were added dried purple California privet berry clusters from the garden, with silk leaf clusters in orange, yellow, and flame stuffed between the boughs. Small glittery orange pumpkins, nestled in the branches, were the final touch.

The overall effect was celebration of a nature-based Thanksgiving, but with a delicious hint of Christmas to come.

Get Ready, Get Set, GO!

Once all traces of Thanksgiving have been stored away, out come the wreaths, garlands, angels, silk poinsettias, artificial trees, glass balls, twinkle lights, Spode Christmas Tree china, and the large stockings, knitted for each of us by Aunt Olga.

These old friends return with a poignant familiarity, like the song, "I'll Be Home for Christmas. "

Holiday Music

My sister starts playing "Santa Baby" in October! Indeed, decorating to Christmas music puts me in the spirit. My husband assembles the tree, while I add ornamentation to rooms that guests will visit. Satellite Radio, the Sirius Pop station, starts playing classical holiday music the day after Thanksgiving.

Kick-off the holiday with a Christmas decorating party. Invite Johnnie Mathis and include cocoa and cookies!

Tree Trimming Party

Tree decorating is just the first of many Christmas holiday entertaining opportunities: a company get-together for cocktails, a holiday tea, Christmas Eve buffet, and Christmas Day dinner.

You might also participate in a soup kitchen or community food drive, to spread holiday cheer.

Signs of Christmas

"It's beginning to look a lot like Christmas," so the song goes.

Excitement and gaiety grow with the placement of each additional, treasured decoration. Even before the tree goes up, a poinsettia, real or silk, plays the part of herald. It won't be long now!

Letter to Santa

There's a lot to be said for asking children to write to Santa, expressing their wish list. If there's something near and dear to their hearts you don't know about, then chances are they will be disappointed Christmas morning. The same goes for adults, too. No one likes to see a crestfallen face or have to take gifts back!

Many extended families only gift the children. Even then, it may be one gift the children all share. Some families give money. A few gift a charity instead of each other. Friends may exchange Christmas ornaments.

Time to Start

I think homemade tokens are the dearest gifts of all. Children want to give gifts, as well. Little ones will need help. Now's the time to get started.

Gifts for Children to Make

1. Box of cookies or fudge
2. Salt box pen and pencil holder
3. Drawing or painting of Nativity scene
4. Small embroidered design in frame
5. Pot holder
6. Tissue and pipe cleaner flowers
7. Child's photo in homemade frame
8. Salt clay sculpture
9. Homemade illustrated storybook
10. Decorative pillow

Christmas Trees

Bring Nature into the Picture

Don't tell the design experts on Home and Garden Television (HGTV), but my personal style is a blend of Romantic Victorian, Country French, Classical (as in Roman), and Early California Garage Sale. However, a unifying principle is to bring the outdoors in and vice a versa.

A dear lady had saved a very large bag of her dried hydrangeas, instead of throwing them away, for her garage sale, priced at 50¢. I snatched them up for multiple uses. They graced our living room tree this year. These huge blossoms seemed to give life to the artificial branches.

***Populate** your home with multiple trees. This year, we put up 4! Have fun with multiples. There's always a way to make room.*

Creating Tree Magic

1. Position your tree in front of a mirror or a window that will reflect the tree lights.

2. Put the tree up on a table. Make that table as large and interesting as possible, with a train track going round and maybe even a little village.

3. Position seating and dining at the level of the tree's base, if possible.

4. Buy an artificial tree that rotates!

Company Holiday Party

Plan dinners with business associates at least 1 ½ months in advance, as everyone's calendar fills quickly; or, invite them just for cocktails.

In our company party invitation, we requested feedback about any dietary considerations guests might have that we could accommodate.

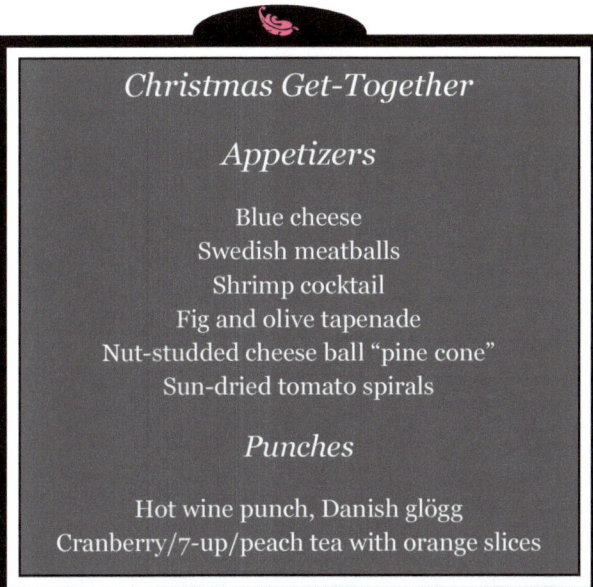

Christmas Get-Together

Appetizers

Blue cheese
Swedish meatballs
Shrimp cocktail
Fig and olive tapenade
Nut-studded cheese ball "pine cone"
Sun-dried tomato spirals

Punches

Hot wine punch, Danish glögg
Cranberry/7-up/peach tea with orange slices

Christmas Punch Bowl

Christmas is one of the those holidays when digging the punch bowl out of the attic is worth the trouble. Parties usually include enough people to make punch an easy and economical solution to supplying drinks over an extended time period. What could be more helpful to a hostess than drinks made ahead?

Sun-dried Tomato Spirals
favorite

1 sheet of puff pastry
1 jar of sun-dried tomato spread
1/4 tsp. garlic powder
1/2 cup crumbled feta cheese
1 egg yolk beaten

Roll out pastry. Slather on spread. Dust with garlic. Sprinkle cheese over spread. Roll up long side to make log. Seal edge with egg yolk. Smear egg yolk over the log. Chill log for 1 hour. Slice log into ¼" slices. Bake on parchment paper on a jelly roll pan at 375° for 12 minutes, turn them over and bake another 12 minutes, until crisp, and serve.

Prepare enough to send "goodie" plates home with your guests.

Plan Ahead

Label serving dishes to remember where everything goes at the last minute. Plan an ice-breaker: pin randomly drawn name tags of famous people on guests' backs. Guests ask yes or no questions of others to determine their name. The winner gets a prize (box of chocolate truffles).

Holiday Bakery

If you are baking cookies, date nut bread loaves in soup cans, or Dresden stollen, display your creations! Use picturesque tins from the 99¢ Only Store or local thrift shop to store cookies and candies  separately, on a crisp paper doily. (Watch out, soft cookies will soften crisp cookies in the same tin.) Located by the front door, they'll be handy for giving.

Christmas Dinner Traditions

Everyone has their special Christmas traditions. Our dear Danish friends, who took us into their family for many Christmases when our parents lived far away, re-enacted their treasured rituals.

Danish Delights

Little north men, wooden red elves with white beards and pointy hats were placed on the mantel. Knitted red yarn bells and tiny plaited paper red and white heart baskets here hung on their tree, around which we all danced in a circle singing carols.

Before dinner, we drank hot spiced red wine, glögg, and sampled crisp, delicate butter cookies. Dinner, around a long table with fresh white tablecloth, began with tiny shrimp in a cloud of whipped cream flavored lightly with mustard on lettuce, open-faced sandwich style.

Dinner followed: roasted goose surrounded by baked apple halves, filled with glistening red currant jelly; caramelized tiny new potatoes, boiled potatoes, and red cabbage.

Dessert was a huge punch bowl full of rice pudding, thick with whipped cream and almonds, over which dark bing cherries in syrup were poured.

We had to keep eating it until someone confessed to having gotten the single whole almond, producing it from their cheek where it had been hidden, until we all groaned from too much pudding! The winner was then gifted with a luscious box of chocolates!

Another charming Danish treat, which we carried on for many years, was to light the tiny candles around a set of brass angels which would spin around, causing their appended needles to tinkle on brass bells below. Everyone gathered, with lights dimmed, to watch the magic happen. Eyes glazed over, mesmerized by sight and sound.

Feature *cut branches of pine, juniper, cypress, cedar, or holly growing on your property inside on your table. Tuck glass balls into the branches to catch the light. Use as filler in vases, wreaths, and garlands that feature contrasting colors and texture. Pair with pyrocanthus, poinsettias, pomegranates, white mums, or red roses. Add billowy ribbons on picks.*

British "Bangers"

This year, our daughter brought her beau home for a Christmas dinner. Thinking that conversation is sometimes awkward around the dinner table, especially between courses, we brought out English crackers, sometimes called poppers, which my daughter had given me for Christmas.

Noisily popping the crackers open enlivened the party, as did the fun of discovering what surprises were inside. We all put on our paper hats, read each other the jokes inside, and demonstrated our toys. It was great fun. Actually, the Brits call sausages bangers!

Christmas Decorating

The Power of Red

Every serving and dining table deserves that trumpet blast of red during the holidays. It's easy to find sources of red. Use: napkins, glasses, plates, tablecloths, candles, poinsettias, cranberries in a vase, tomatoes and red peppers on appetizer plates, ribbon, wrapping paper, tinsel, stockings, runners, glass bead ropes, furniture throws, pillows, yuletide camellias, roses, foil around plants, and aprons, shirts, sweaters, robes, dresses, and skirts around people!

Large pre-made red velvet bows are a good investment, when acquired at after-Christmas sales. A large red bow against a green wreath, real or artificial, is hard to beat for eye-popping-appeal, red and green being exciting complementary colors.

Red bows also give that wow factor to lamp posts and garage doors (with or without the wreath). Inside, a red bow can dress an entire room for Christmas, placed on a side board or pantry door or above a hearth or below a T.V. Five or seven are the perfect counterpoints to a garland of fir draped in swags down a banister.

The Softness of Silver

My family gave me three large mercury glass balls and a glass candlestick with cranberry candle. They thoughtfully included several feet of ½" silky velvet cranberry ribbon and a yard of fine ruby red satin ribbon to hang the balls. I had the fun of playing with all these resources to create my hearth display. Decorating supplies make great gifts!

To add more silvery sheen, I gathered all my oldest silver glass balls into a crystal bowl, on top of which I placed a sparkling red-feathered cardinal.

Silver pine cones. Skewer a dozen large pine cones with long eye hooks, used as handles to dip the cones into silver paint and drain. Hang the cones from a banister, at intervals along a garland.

What's unexpected? Place one on the outside of each step going upstairs. Hang them from hooks framing an archway or on the branches of a bare tree outside or inside, on a large potted branch.

New Year's Eve

Even if your Christmas decorations are still up on Dec. 31, make an effort to decorate a party table unique to New Year's Eve.

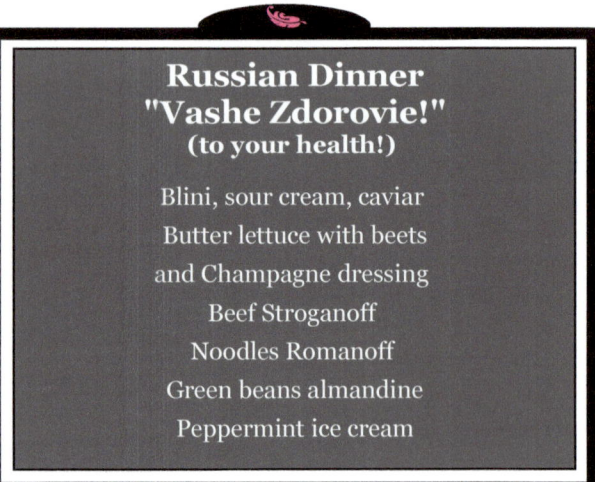

**Russian Dinner
"Vashe Zdorovie!"
(to your health!)**

Blini, sour cream, caviar
Butter lettuce with beets
and Champagne dressing
Beef Stroganoff
Noodles Romanoff
Green beans almandine
Peppermint ice cream

Creative Centerpieces

Maybe you have a Father Time (bearded gnome) or Baby New Year (kewpie doll with top hat) to use as centerpieces? I group all things celestial at different heights: hourglass, blue mercury glass vase with star-studded ball stopper, blue planetarium tube, wizard, crystal ball on brass stand, gyroscope, and Styrofoam ball covered in gold clock paper!

Positive tarot cards are hidden under each plate. People choose which seat to take and lift their plates to find their messages from the Universe! Dinner music is Holtz's "The Planets."

Listen to old rock and roll, sing, bang on all the rhythm band instruments you have or just spoons and pots. Parade through the house, until it's time to toast the New Year!

Gold, Silver, and Champagne

Of course, gold and silver cardboard hats or feathery headbands with glitter are requisite, as are coils of streamers and noise makers.

Forget the confetti! It's too much trouble to clean up, unless it's sprinkled on the tablecloth, rather than thrown into the air!

Champagne and sparkling cider on ice with plastic or glass flutes in waiting build anticipation for the stroke of midnight.

Create Drama

1. 11:50, invite guests to write a trouble to be rid of, then toss the folded note paper into the lit fireplace.
2. 11:55, turn down the lights and ask guests to light a candle in anticipation of a bright New Year.
3. 11:58, ask guests to make a wish for the New Year and blow out their candle at 12:00. Flip on the lights and toast!

New Year's Day

If your family rang in the New Year, sleeping in is their first order of the day. After that, help family ease into the late morning with muffins, fruit, and strong coffee. Watch a rerun of the Pasadena Tournament of Roses Parade. Children will want to say which is their favorite float. If you have one or more little girls in the house, make a ceremony of crowning them as your "Rose Princesses," with dollar store tiaras or garlands of roses you've made. Little boys might be given a Nerf football and named Rose Bowl quarterbacks of the day!

Day of Roses

Take your party cue from the Rose Parade and Rose Bowl football game. Rise early to surprise your family and any houseguests by making fresh muffins. Have at the ready and set out everything with roses on it that you've gathered the day before to decorate the T.V. room. Most people will be expecting things to be set up for guys to watch football. That doesn't mean you have to have football-shaped dip and chip bowls out, though! Between or during games, ladies might choose to watch an old romance on another T.V., like *Bed of Roses*; or if the football hoopla gets to be too much, *War of the Roses*!

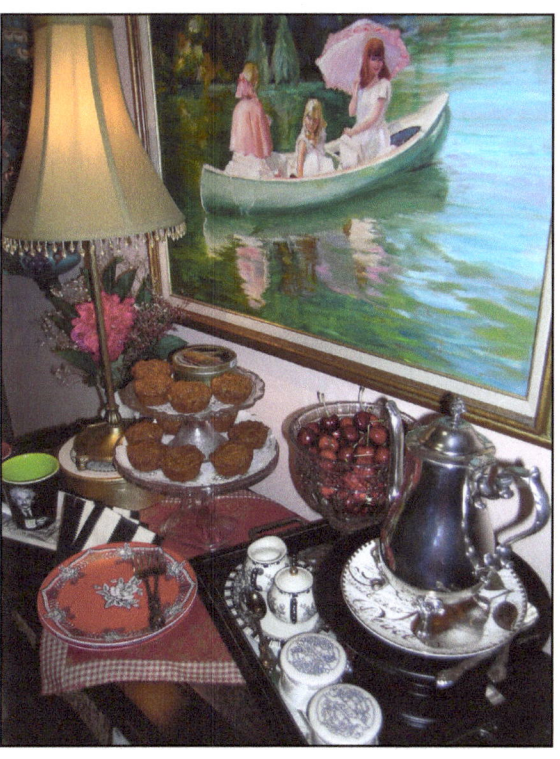

Finger Food

Ruben half sandwiches
(grilled pastrami and Swiss cheese on rye)

Rachel sandwiches
(cream cheese and lox on baby bagel)

Deli pickles and green tomatoes

Strawberry- topped cheesecake

Service Table Tips

1. Layer tablecloths.
2. Sew fabric remnants together to make table toppers and runners.
3. Use plate holders as serving trays, showing off pretty mismatched china.
4. Include a plant and flowers to bring the freshness of the garden in (or silk).
5. Cast a warm glow over the table with a small lamp or multiple candles.
6. Remember to include silverware and napkins.

Winter Wonderland

Winter White

If you happen to live east of California, say in the cities of Chicago or Buffalo, enough with the white already! In snow country, I'd have plenty of warm lighting in the rooms where family would gather most, colorful overstuffed furniture by a cozy fireside, shots of red in mufflers and throws and tablecloths, a red sled propped by the front door, and a small tree with pine cones and white fairy lights in a red bucket near the hearth. Outside my window, with a length of bright red wool, I'd hang a pine cone slathered in peanut butter and bird seed to see what critters I might attract. There would be a red ceramic pitcher at the ready for cocoa and a jar full of oat cookies.

In California the promise of spring comes on January 2nd, when I resume my morning walks in the neighborhood marveling at the pansies, poppies, snapdragons, and irises in full bloom!

Winter Decorating

1. Choose a theme from storybooks, fairy tales, musicals, and operas.

2. Take a world tour by changing your table for Italian, French, Spanish, and Japanese meals.

3. Give family meals ambiance: use candles and music!

4. Be a stage director! Set up an area for musical jamming and theatrical improvisations.

Swan Lake Theme

What can possibly replace the bright beauty of Christmas? The quiet beauty of nature.

Where the Victorian Christmas tree had been, I put a lamp that glows in warm gold colors. Next to that is my swan made of birch and cornstalks. She's nestled in a woven basket filled with sprays of lavender. Tucking dried pink statice into the lavender was the final touch. Always stand back from your creations. Does it look or feel complete? Play Goldilocks: experiment by adding and subtracting, until it's "just right."

Group objects in odd numbers. You'll find they are so much more attractive than in even numbers.

Kid Decorators

Children learn by doing, choosing their own room colors and fabrics. My daughter helped decorate her bedroom with her toys. After Christmas is a perfect time to "redecorate" to feature new books, stuffed animals, and dolls. A little girl's bedroom is like a dollhouse on a grander scale. It should be fun to play house and have tea parties in it! Bunk beds make great pirate ships, castles, and double-deck buses.

Winter Blooms

Forced Bulbs

Large groupings are more dramatic than a single pot. Try "Mother-in-law's Tongue" with amaryllis and paperwhites in a large rectangular basket. This grouping on a library table or desk piled high with books and a good reading lamp invites inquiry. What's growing here? Install a comfy chair and ottoman for passers-by to tarry awhile. Invite discovery.

To force bulbs, start them indoors before their natural bloom. Bulb roots planted in loose soil or in a bed of pebbles and water will quickly send up green shoots. Some bulbs require refrigeration (away from tomatoes) before planting, like fragrant hyacinth. Perfumed paperwhites don't require chilling. Bulbs make great gifts.

Collect *inspiring decorating books and cookbooks at yard sales and your library's used book store for just a dollar or two. Recent decorating magazines are just 5/$1. Dream through them in the winter months for ideas to implement come Spring.*

Pussy Willows

Pussy willows bought at a flower market or cut from a bush will grow (even if dried out), when put in water. Their soft little toes beg to be touched. Cut about a yard long and display in a large clear vase, just so the ends sit in the water. They bring the miracle of growth into the house. Our family likes to watch leaves sprout from the branches, before they're planted outside.

Amaryllis Care

1. Plant bulb roots in loose soil in snug pot; water when dry; rotate bloom stalk; cut when withered.
2. After frost, water bulb outside through summer; cut leaves; store in cool dry place.
3. Repeat process mid-October.

Martin Luther King Day

How do you decorate for this newest holiday? For me, the Calla lily is a perfect symbol of Dr. King's purity of spirit and purpose. I'd display a lily next to an encyclopedia opened to his photo and commemorative newspaper articles. It's also a fitting time, during Black History Month, to pay tribute to other famous and not-so-famous African American men and women who helped build our country and prod it to live up to its principles.

School Programs

It's good to know that our children are growing up with a much different point of view than that which prevailed in *our* youth. My daughter's elementary school was visited by "Coretta Scott King," that is an actress portraying her. She told the stories of her husband; the famous ball-player, Jackie Robinson; and George Washington Carver, who saved the South with peanut production and food preservation technology.

Harriet Tubman was portrayed, too, dramatically re-enacting her courageous efforts to free slaves. Bringing these people to life for young children makes a lasting impression.

African Cuisine

This is a great day to celebrate all things that come to our melting pot of a country from African heritage. Time Life put out a series of cookbooks featuring the great cuisines and cultures of the world. My mother-in-law and I put together a wonderful African meal from their *Cooking of Africa*.

Amaze your family with the contributions of these famous people. Biographies are a wonderful way to remember. Read them to your children. Reading together allows you to underscore heroic achievements with your own words.

Splendors of Africa

Hummus
Chicken with cashew nuts
Cabbage rolls stuffed with spicy lamb
Yellow rice with raisins
Date chutney
Cucumber sambal
Flat bread
Molded tangerine and ginger custard

Frederick Douglass

Mother painted a beautiful portrait for an African American friend of hers, a dedicated teacher, who revered this great man for his work to abolish slavery and give women the vote.

If recipes from Africa sound too challenging, go for Creole creations, Caribbean jerk meats, and good old-fashioned southern cooking. The exuberance of these wonderful cooking styles comes from their African influence. If nothing else, discover and relish "soul food."

Chinese New Year

Even without Chinese ancestors, you can still celebrate Chinese New Year! It's a great excuse to make Chinese food and bring out the paper lanterns, fans, bamboo plant, chopsticks, and all your Asian collections! Greet your guests with, "Gung Hay Fat Choy!" Wear your silk pajamas, a silk jacket or robe, or something red, the color of good luck.

Asian Dining Room

Long runners of Asian patterned fabric are easy to make. Or, use long woven mats directly on your wood or glass-top table or over a red tablecloth. Black and gold are perfect accent colors for plates, trays, and napkins. Add fresh or silk orchids or use wooden kitchen gods and colorful ginger jars. Chopsticks add authenticity. If you have Chinese fans or

dolls, place them on serving tables. Buy fortune cookies and buy or make almond cookies to finish off your menu. Provide individual teapots from a restaurant supply store or one large teapot. If you're pressed for time, order Chinese take-out and put the cartons on the table. Otherwise, have fun trying new recipes.

Sensory Delights

Chinese music ("Silk Road" is a beautiful suite), incense, and exotic fruits, such as kiwi, lichee nuts, kumquats, and Asian pears, add mystery. A book of Confucian proverbs is intriguing on a side table, as is the Time Life *Cooking of China* cookbook, open to the story of how rice is grown.

Chinese Banquet

Wonton soup

Spareribs

Salad (with Girard's Oriental Dressing)

Peking pancakes

Fried rice

Mongolian grill

Cashew chicken

Cream pudding with mandarin oranges and fresh raspberries

Invite *guests to come in costume. Entertain them with their Chinese birth year horoscopes.*

Peking Pancakes
favorite

1 cup flour
½ tsp. salt
1/3 cup boiling water
4 strips crisp bacon, crumbled
reserved bacon fat
2 spring onions, thinly sliced
3 tbsp. sesame seeds
1 tbsp. oil

Mix flour, salt, and water. Knead 3 minutes. Cover. Let rest ½ hr. Roll out to 8" x 16" on floured board. Brush on bacon fat. Cut 8 2" strips. Sprinkle on onion. Roll up strips, turn on side, and flatten. Sprinkle seeds on both sides. Fry in oil, 3 min. per side. Serve hot.

Paint *art especially for your ethnic parties. Look for inspiration in "National Geographic" magazines.*

Valentine's Day

Sweetheart Suite

True, Valentine's Day might appropriately command some special sweetheart decorations in the master bedroom. We'll not go there in this column, except to recommend fresh flowers, fresh soaps, displaying collections of perfume bottles, pulling out the honeymoon lingerie, favorite music, bath salt and bubbles, fluffy spa robes, massage lotions, and chocolates on the pillows! Favorite photos in silver frames on side tables, illumined in candlelight, are romantic, too.

This is the season of lovers, Cupid, hearts, flowers, chocolates, hand-made cards, paper doilies, old lace, wedding veils, and bride and groom wedding cake toppers. And, once again, the color red prevails as the color of family, friendship, love, passion, and fire!

Focal Points

In my house, there are certain surfaces whose decorations change only with the season. While winter decorations remain on the hall desk and living room library table after Christmas through St. Patrick's Day, the dining and family room focal points are redecorated for each holiday.

A generous mantle, where family and friends gather, invites updated displays, as do dining and serving tables.

Include *objects that are meaningful to your family and friends. Seeing those objects come out at the appropriate holiday builds a sense of continuity, tradition, belonging, anticipation, and value.*

Breakfast in Bed

Hot homemade waffles

Butter & syrup in little pitchers

Crisp bacon

Chocolate-dipped strawberries

Mimosas (orange juice & champagne)

Valentine Party

Valentine's Day is, of course, about dining out with your sweetheart. However, it's also the perfect time to celebrate your love of family, friends, and especially children with an afternoon tea party.

Afternoon Tea

Cupcakes sprinkled with hearts

Strawberry Bavarian crème

Tea sandwiches

Scones

Latticed cherry pie

Sweetened, delicious, ruby red hibiscus tea

Valentine Party Ideas

1. Kids love to decorate heart cookies.

2. Guests young at heart can play secret admirer with fellow guests. Print all guest names on separate slips for a drawing. Each guest creates a Valentine for the person whose name they drew, using craft supplies you provide.

3. Set up a croquet Wonderland in your yard or the park. Invite the Queen of Hearts, in costume, to tally points earned to reward with red-foil covered chocolate hearts. Use markers and file folders to make playing card wickets.

Tokens of Love

On Valentine's Day, pull out the stops! Don't be subtle; be out there in your original expressions of ardor. Plan surprises. It may take several to get your message across! Play "our song" morning and night. Pull out, blow up, or especially frame and place favorite old photos of you and your sweetheart with a love note. The shower, his bed pillow, car seat, or briefcase might work. Fix his favorite meal and dessert, even if it's a hamburger and apple pie. Wear a short red skirt or new nightgown. Resurrect letters or poems to share or write new ones. Drive somewhere different to take a walk, holding hands.

Send tokens of love in your children's school lunch bags. Write a love note, saying what makes them so special. Draw a picture of your family on the note with hearts all around it. Tie a red bow around the sandwich inside; include a Valentine cookie; add a pretty Valentine napkin or paper doily. Make the day special, starting at breakfast. Deliver their plates with a kiss on each cheek. End the day with big hugs and the words, "I love you."

Take Time to Listen

Life can be so hectic. On the old Newly Wed game show, the bride and groom were asked questions about each other that they didn't get right. What's his or her favorite color? Who is his favorite female movie star? What is he especially proud of having done? Sweetheart, child, or parent—how well do you really know your loved one? Ask questions about likes and dislikes, dreams and best memories, favorite songs and favorite places at home. Repeat the answers you hear, so your loved one knows you heard.

Homemade Valentines

Two of the best Valentines I ever received were made by my daughter. Each was a ceramic heart, made in grade school, which could be hung by a ribbon.

President's Day

Every presidential election year inspires me to celebrate President's Day (especially, if my candidate wins!). Have you memories of cutting out Washington and Lincoln silhouettes for the holiday? How many presidents can you name? Consider giving a prize at dinner to the person who can write down the names of the most presidents. Children might actually do very well at this! How about a 3-D puzzle of the Capitol building in Washington, D. C. as first prize, unassembled, of course!

Ask who, at the dinner table, each guest would elect as president. If there's consensus, who would that president appoint to his cabinet, from among the guests, and why? It's a fun, teaching moment and can get diehards really going!

Invite your children to build a house of Lincoln logs or hot-glued twigs (with your help) for your centerpiece. Have them try to read by candlelight, as Abe did.

Flags, Flags, and More Flags

Whether it's President's Day or Memorial Day, Veteran's Day or Labor Day, Flag Day or the granddaddy of them all, the 4th of July, flags are *de rigeur* for national holidays.

Ephemera

Even if you are only celebrating the occasion with a special family dinner, it's fun to display campaign buttons, banners, and poster collections.

Because we made a contribution to our candidate's campaign, we received a beautiful embossed invitation to his and the vice president's inauguration.

Framed and featured on a side table in the dining room, it makes us feel we're a part of something great, on a national scale. Did you know you can vote on issues before Congress at www.congress.org?

American Country

Down Home Fare

Shrimp cocktail

Succotash salad

Dutch oven chicken and homemade noodles

Sweet potato biscuits

Cherry Pie

Yam Bams (Biscuits)
favorite

1 cup heavy cream
2 tbsp. lemon juice
1 1/4 cup baked, mashed yam
3 cups flour
1½ tbsp. baking powder
1 ½ tsp. salt
1 tbsp. sugar
1 stick cold butter minced
apricot jam and butter

Set oven at 475°. Combine cream and lemon. Prepare yam and add to cream. Combine dry ingredients. Cut in butter. Mix with yam and cream. Pat dough ½" thick on floured board. Cut into stars or rounds. Bake on sheet pan for 15 min. Serve hot with butter and apricot jam.

Read about the life of John Adams, by David McCullough, a wonderful writer. Become the presidential expert in your family.

Rent a DVD on President Washington's life to watch after dinner with your family.

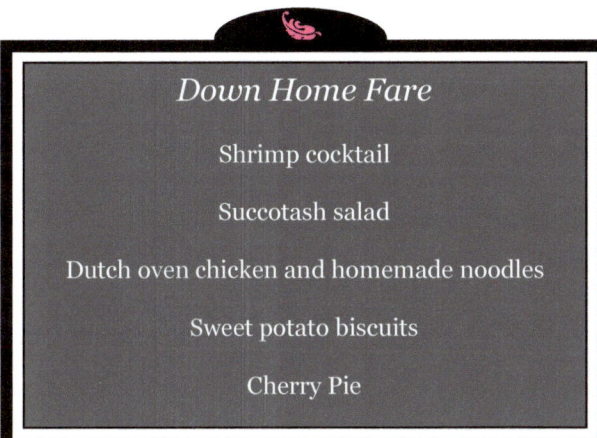

Rachel's Cherry Cream Cheese Pie
favorite

1 3 oz. pkg. cream cheese softened

½ cup powdered sugar

1 pint of heavy cream whipped stiff

1 can cherry pie filling

1 baked pie crust cooled
(preferably made with oil or butter)

Combine cream cheese and sugar. Fold in whipped cream. Smooth mixture in baked pie shell. Top with 1 can cherry pie filling. Chill before serving. This cream cheese filling is also delicious in crepes, topped with sweetened berries or peaches or spread on date nut bread, with a little spoonful of seedless red raspberry jam.

St. Patrick's Day

Everyone can share in Irish Day who has a bit of blarney in them! Or, whoever likes to sing, dance a jig, and tell stories whilst downing an Irish Coffee!

Going Green

Every shade of green works, especially emerald green. So, if you are short on leprechauns and green foil shamrocks, just look around the house for anything that says nature. Gather up live and silk green plants, rustic baskets, pots of violets, little tins that look like cottages, and all the lace doilies you can find. You've got the makings of fairytales and folklore.

If you want a bit more of the Irish look, check out dollar bins for a green cellophane bowler hat. Ropes of metallic green beads look beautiful in moss at the base of a topiary—quite like leprechaun land.

Going Gold

Gather up all things gold to incorporate into your displays, too. Keep your eye out for gold filigreed cookie tins at antique stores, flea markets, garage sales, and grandma's pantry. They work well stacked to add height and brilliance.

__Hide__ chocolate coins on March 17th in gold foil outdoors and in. Tell the kids the leprechaun left them behind in his haste to get away before being caught!

Going White

Make generous use of lace, even if it's not Irish. Against dark wood, lace makes a striking contrast for highlighting your collectibles: frogs, geese, ducks, moss in baskets with little flowers, wooden toys, Irish cookbooks, and green pitchers!

Ethnic Parties

1. Keep a cookbook of world cuisine for reference. I love Shiela Lukins' *All Around the World Cookbook* and the *New York Times International Cookbook*.

2. Pick up ethnic-looking tablecloths.

3. Think outside your normal décor. A few rustic clay items and basketry can work with many ethnic themes.

4. Start a collection of ethnic music.

5. Research the culture, so you can share what makes it unique.

6. Shop for your party at the appropriate "mom and pop" ethnic market in your area. Include their authentic prepared foods. If there are none, check World Market, i.e., Cost Plus.

7. Take inspiration from ethnic festivals in your area.

8. Be aware of and use typical ethnic colors

Irish Flair

Setting the Table

A freshly ironed white tablecloth is the perfect backdrop for an Irish dinner for family and/or friends. Green napkins, gold chargers under white and green plates, green glass goblets, gold candles in dark wood candleholders will create the right impression. Cut out green shamrocks to place on the cloth. Your centerpiece should carry out the theme. If you want to go all out, make leprechaun clothes to dress an old doll in and seat him upon a basket turned upside down, surround by ferns with chocolate gold coins tucked in and around the plant. Crystal, Irish Crystal, in particular, is the finishing touch. Either lively pipe or haunting harp music add an air of authenticity.

Irish Feast

Irish stew or corned beef

Boiled cabbage

Steamed golden potatoes

Boiled cauliflower and broccoli

Luxurious béchamel sauce, enriched with cheddar cheese

Homemade Irish soda bread

Ande's crisp mint and chocolate wafers

Irish coffee (strong sweetened coffee, Irish whiskey, and whipping cream)

Toast

may the road rise up to meet you,
may the wind be always at your back,
may the sun shine warm upon your face,
and the rain fall soft upon your fields,
and until we meet again,
may God hold you in the palm of His hand....

--Author unknown

Annie's Famous Irish Soda Bread
favorite

3 cups flour
2/3 cup sugar
1 tblsp. baking powder
1 tsp. baking soda
1 tsp. salt
2 eggs
1 3/4 cups buttermilk
2 tblsp. melted butter
1 1/2 cup raisins

Preheat oven to 350°. Grease and flour 2 cake pans. Mix dry & wet ingredients. Divide batter into the 2 pans. Bake for 30 minutes, until test toothpick comes out clean. Remove from pans and cool on a rack or serve warm with butter.

Spring Time

Spring blossoms show up the last week in February, if California has had a bit of rain and temperatures in the 70s. Even if you live in the snow belt, you can still change your color palette with the calendar. Retire the jewel tones for pastels. Put away the amaryllis, bring out silk tulips, daffodils, hyacinth, freesia, and lilacs, until nature provides. Perhaps she'll take her cue from you!

If you've never planted bulbs in the fall for spring flowering, give it a try. It's easy.

Wreaths Say Welcome

Consider changing your front door wreath with each season. Go with evergreens for winter, flowers for spring, berries for summer, and oak leaves for fall, or variations thereof.

Entry Way Set Design

On either side of your front door, change décor to announce the new season. If you have plants near the front door, switch them around with others in the garden that are now in bloom. Or, plant spring flowers around the base of potted plants too large to move. Poppies, pansies, snapdragons, and especially primroses—even just a few of one kind—will raise your visitor's and family members' spirits.

Plant a lilac bush in your yard. My white lilacs do best. The colder the winter, the better. Some advise putting ice cubes around the base of the bush a few times in January. If you can't grow them, buy them in season with peonies at Trader Joe's for heady fragrance.

Surprise the person opening the front door with a spring vignette. A round table with floor length tablecloth in your favorite color, pink, yellow, periwinkle, or lavender invites notice. Adorn the table with favorite floral motifs: an art book open to a spring scene, a bouquet of flowers, a nosegay oil painting in a gold frame. Arrange the treasures in something unexpected, perhaps a cabinet or tiered plate stand.

Fresh Start

Bring the Garden Inside

My parents surprised me with a little Mother Nature gnome, who stands watch in the garden most of the year. But in she comes to grace the hall desk next to a floral lamp, which replaces the metal, marble, and leather version usually out during the winter months.

Bring the garden indoors. Pots of flowers in sunny windows make people smile. It's time to plant seeds. Start them in your kitchen window. Tape the seed packets on chopsticks staked in the pots until the plants grow.

> *Spring Dinner Party*
>
> Steamed asparagus
>
> Meyer lemon and butter dipping sauce
>
> Ham and artichoke crepes
>
> Roasted baby new potatoes
>
> Strawberry shortcake

Baskets, Linens, and Produce

Easter baskets are especially appropriate to spring decorating. They can show up in bathrooms, guest rooms, the kitchen, and dining room to hold essentials. If you normally store goods in boxes or tins or glass jars, think about trading those out for baskets lined with fresh linens in spring colors. Now is an especially good time to use hand-embroidered tea towels and pillowcases.

Nothing quite excites the appetite, other than delicious aromas, as an abundant display of produce. Take those lovely fruits and veggies out of their bags and fill glass bowls and baskets instead.

Spring Cleaning

Freshen the look of bedding. Open windows, if you can. Pull back drapes. Let more light flood in. Use a new sponge. Open a new bar of soap! Change your outlook and wardrobe! Announce the arrival of spring with new collars for your dog and cat.

***Paint** flowers. Start with a small cluster of posies and be sure to frame your work. Put it out where you can enjoy it. If you have never painted, take a beginning class at the local high school or recreation center in the evenings. It's great fun!*

April in Paris

Even if you've never been to Paris, you can still appreciate the City of Light and Love. My idea of spring is the experience of Paris. Call me romantic! It's such a lovely city of light-colored, gracious old buildings with wrought iron balconies. Parks abound with fine gravel paths and inviting benches. Café windows sparkle in a spring shower. Patisseries pull you in by the nose to sample their delectable pastries.

Though my kitchen cabinets are a honey-colored oak, the freestanding cabinets I've added are black. I even went so far as to paint the freestanding stove island cabinet black. The framed aperitif pictures on cabinets came from calendars.

Make your own coffee bar turn-table, then stack 1 or 2 cake stands in the center to hold a huge vase of flowers, a statue, or more syrups.

To create that feeling at home, I covered my old floral couch in the kitchen with black and white ticking (actually a sheet set from Target). Then added black pillows, toile pillows, and panels at the windows made from toile scraps and black dish cloths.

A designer trick to try: combine one black or white furry or shaggy pillow with your print throw pillows for an unexpected, decorator look. Black and white always add a note of elegance, like tuxedos!

Tall tin buckets or wicker plant stands work well to hold sprays of spring blossoms. I also have a garden Eiffel Tower replica in black wire on the kitchen coffee table, between piles of favorite decorating and cookbooks. I love to hang out here with a cup of coffee brewed by my husband in his café bar!

A Parisian Soiree

> **Share,** *ask guests to present their art, poetry, favorite cookbook or wine, special knowledge of current events, or latest gardening triumph!*
>
> *A soiree is a gathering of elegant, refined individuals generally held in the evening. It's an event designed to inspire and illuminate those fortunate to attend.*

Collect Chic Serving Pieces

It used to be the fashion to match all one's china. Now, it's okay, even more stylish, to combine pieces chosen because they complement your dinnerware. Choose pieces that fit with the color, texture, size, and character of your china, but do not match them exactly.

Different size rectangular white china platters are also very versatile. I use my large one to corral my bottles of oil, vinegar, and wine that I use everyday for cooking. When I need it for service, I just remove the bottles to the counter.

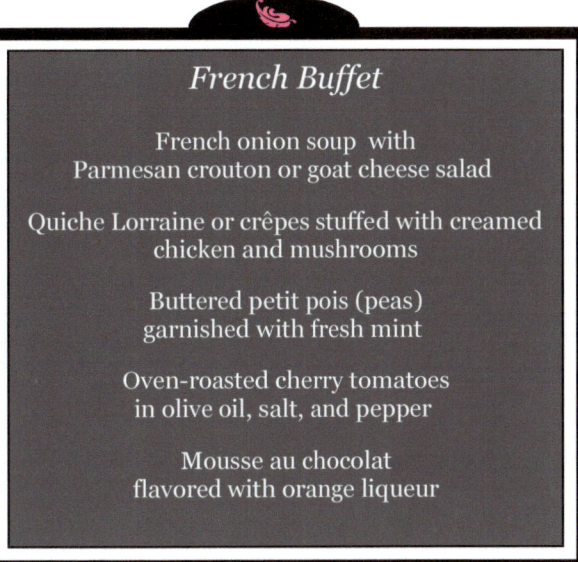

French Buffet

French onion soup with
Parmesan crouton or goat cheese salad

Quiche Lorraine or crêpes stuffed with creamed chicken and mushrooms

Buttered petit pois (peas)
garnished with fresh mint

Oven-roasted cherry tomatoes
in olive oil, salt, and pepper

Mousse au chocolat
flavored with orange liqueur

Salade avec Chêvre

favorite

1 goat cheese log
1 egg white whipped with fork
2 cups bread crumbs (ciabatta)
2 tblsp. butter
2 tblsp. olive or vegetable oil
Mixed salad greens
Girard's Champagne Dressing

Slice cheese into ½" rounds with dental floss. Dip in egg white, then coat in bread crumbs. Chill for ½ hour. Just before serving, fry cheese in melted butter and oil. Serve on greens tossed with dressing.

Easter

My husband's family celebrates Easter in the traditional Byzantine Catholic tradition. A basket is laden with Paska, a cheese bread, hard-boiled eggs, ham, horseradish, nut rolls, and delicate jam-filled cookies. Over the basket, a fresh white linen is placed. This is taken to midnight mass for the priest's blessing.

Traditions

Easter meant new spring outfits for the girls in my family to wear to church, with crisp straw hats, banded in black grosgrain ribbon. Just like anticipating the packages left by Santa, we girls would burst from our bedrooms to see what the Easter Bunny had left for us. Easter egg hunts, whether outdoors or in, with real eggs or plastic eggs filled with candy, followed for us kids.

One of the best Easter egg hunts we ever had was designed to include adults. The competition was fierce to see who could collect the most eggs and thus win a special prize. Older children enjoy a hunt, when dollar bills are put into plastic eggs.

Egg Decoration

At several Easter parties we've set up an egg-dying station in the kitchen, complete with egg-shells ready for waxing and dipping. Glass cups held the die baths (be sure to have vinegar on hand with your Paas Egg Dye Kit from the market).

Push a pin with a metal head into a pencil eraser. This becomes a stylus. Dip the pin head into the pool of melted wax of a lighted candle to draw flowers or other shapes. Then submerge the egg into a light-colored dye to soak for awhile. Waxed areas will not take the dye. Remove the egg, make further wax decorations and submerge the egg in another, darker color. Repeat until your creation is finished. Gently dry the egg, scrape off the wax, and polish it.

Easter Traditions

Giant Yellow Easter Egg
favorite "Cirak"

12 eggs, slightly beaten

1 qt. whole milk

1 tsp. salt

Mix altogether in saucepan. Heat over low flame until it curdles and looks like scrambled eggs (be careful not to scorch!). Pour mixture into cheesecloth and tie tightly, forming into large egg shape. Hang over faucet to drain for 3 hours. Wrap in plastic. Refrigerate to keep from spoiling. To serve, slice like cheese with salt.

Easter Treats

Although children love to find their own (store-bought) Easter baskets, adults need to be indulged, too!

See's Candies makes wonderful foil covered bunny chocolates. Place one, as a party favor, at each guest's table setting, if the budget allows. Otherwise, the local drug store, Big Lots, or WalMart will have Little Peeps or marshmallow bunnies covered in chocolate.

Jelly beans, colored eggs, cellophane grass, flowers, little animals can all go into a nature-based centerpiece for the table. Make a butter lamb: push butter through a garlic press to make "wool."

Keep the completed eggs over the years. Store them in a large glass jar for safety. We bring our collection out to wonder over each Easter. It's fun to recognize everyone's very distinct styles.

Eastern European ladies are famous for their intricately decorated eggs. Books are available at most libraries with instructions on how to create masterpieces, using dyes, homemade from red and brown onion skins and beets.

Easter Bread

Greek Easter bread recipes call for an egg, dyed red with beet juice, to be embedded in the center of the dough. The raw egg within the shell bakes with the bread. The result is lovely presented in a linen-lined basket at the dinner table.

Display *left over white egg shells in a wire basket year-round, as if you just gathered them. Spray them in the sink to drain, if they get dusty.*

One treasure that we bring out each Easter is a Victorian puzzle of connected cubes that can be rearranged to show old-fashioned Easter scenes. Large papier mâché eggs halved for holding goodies are great finds. Although I have only found one, I'd like to add another each year to build a collection.

Outdoor Decorating

Create Garden Rooms

1. Arrange furniture into intimate settings for 2 to 4 people.

2. Define the setting with outdoor flooring: deck, rugs, tile, gravel, sand.

3. If you like motion, install different kinds of swings for kids and adults.

4. Group plants around or on either side of setting at different elevations.

5. Repeat colors and textures in the different settings to tie them all together.

6. Plant fragrant flowers, vines and bushes near seating, such as: jasmine, honeysuckle, and gardenias.

Decorate Your Garden

1. Flank a fixed French door with a tall planter for outdoor and indoor beauty.

2. Plant a dwarf fruit tree in an oversized pot on casters to follow the sun.

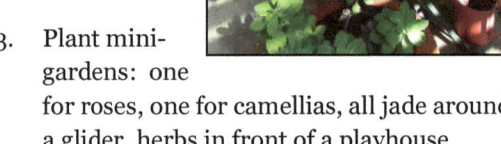

3. Plant mini-gardens: one for roses, one for camellias, all jade around a glider, herbs in front of a playhouse.

4. Use trellises, topiaries, weathered pots, urns, sundials, and attractive lighting.

5. Include sculptures: animals, birds, fairies, gnomes, Grecian columns.

6. Change out faded patio furniture cushions with giant pillow slips you make.

7. Mix furniture for interest: metal, wood, wicker, concrete, and twigs.

Cinco de Mayo

Why celebrate the 5th of May, Mexico's defeat of France? In Southern California, we pay tribute to the region's Spanish and Indian heritage! Who doesn't love tortilla chips, salsa, and margaritas? It's the perfect excuse to indulge in Hispanic culture, reveling in all its color, music, history, and luscious Latin flavors! ¡Olé! People revel in May Day the world over. Summer's coming!

Stripes, Fringe, and Ball Tassels

Fringed, creamy white, "slubby-nubby-textured" fabrics shout "south of the border," especially if they sport a few brightly-colored stripes. Serapes, ponchos, sombreros, huaraches (sandals), full skirts in bands of bright colors—pull them out of storage and start decorating!

Hang them on the walls of your party room and drape them over furniture. A sombrero makes a perfect centerpiece.

Terra Cotta

The earthy tones of Mexico, siennas, ochres, blue agave, and cactus patch green provide a soothing background for splashes of bright yellow, blue, and red. Layer tablecloths, placemats, napkins and clay pots exuberantly!

Olvera Street

Create L.A.'s old Mexico street of shops in your own backyard. Display all your collectibles, create a huge buffet of spicy dishes, and keep the music and beverages flowing. Be glad to be outside!

Match *zesty Mariachi music on one of the Spanish radio stations with lots of lemons, limes, chilies, tomatoes, and avocados. Bring out the maracas and castanets and play along! Play music by the Tijuana Brass.*

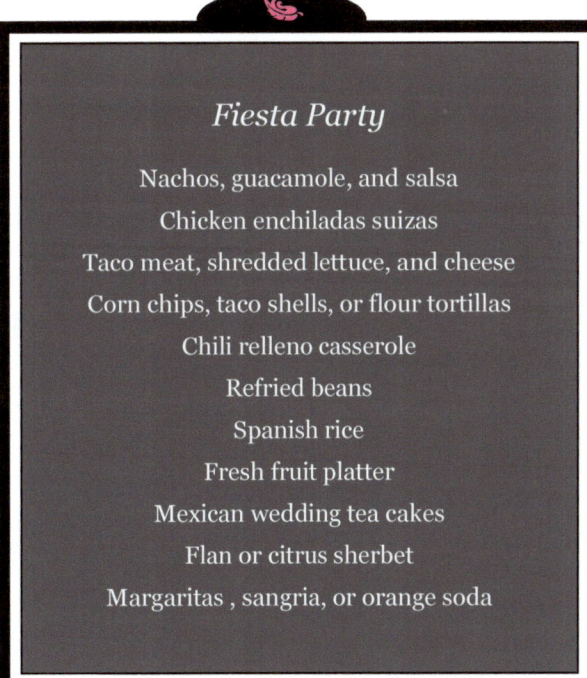

Fiesta Party

Nachos, guacamole, and salsa
Chicken enchiladas suizas
Taco meat, shredded lettuce, and cheese
Corn chips, taco shells, or flour tortillas
Chili relleno casserole
Refried beans
Spanish rice
Fresh fruit platter
Mexican wedding tea cakes
Flan or citrus sherbet
Margaritas, sangria, or orange soda

Mother's Day

The second Sunday in May is devoted to mothers, grandmothers, great-grandmothers, mothers-in-law, and all those ladies who care so tenderly for their surrogate children, their beloved pets! Though moms like to be remembered for their particular ways of indulging their families, this day is also about pampering them.

Breakfast in Bed

Dads have the special duty of helping their children pull together a breakfast tray for Mom. And, they are responsible for getting the kids to clean up afterward!

If your child has ever been treated to breakfast in bed, then he or she will have some idea of how to go about it. Be sure to have fixings noticeably available!

Spa Treatment

Setting fresh towels out, pretty soap and bubble bath, a fluffy white terry cloth robe; playing soothing music; lighting a fragrant candle; placing favorite ladies' magazines on a side table; providing a tray of her favorite chilled juice and a decadent chocolate; filling a vase full of fragrant flowers—all of this presented in a softly lighted bathroom, with the promise of privacy for a full hour, these are very thoughtful gifts for the busy Mom.

When Mom is Far Away

Mothers most love hearing from their children. A card is lovely with a hand-written message, and a phone call allows her to wrap herself around that dear voice.

Sharing even a photocopy of your favorite picture of you with your Mom will touch her deeply. Reminding her of what you miss about her and treasure most when you have time together will dissolve her into tears of joy or peals of laughter.

Going Out for Lunch or Dinner

By all means, do take Mom out to a restaurant for her special day. Do not expect her to make the family meal! Moms too easily commit themselves to cooking, because they are making the meal special for their mothers and mothers-in-law.

Mother's Day Brunch

Make-ahead Mom's Meal

Chicken salad croissants

Roast beef and onion croissants

Mediterranean grilled veggie ciabattas

Homemade potato salad

Watermelon

Ranch and cucumber dip

Potato chips, macadamias

Cranberry orange relish

Asparagus in Champagne dressing

Rhubarb and strawberry crisp

Caramel turtle ice cream

favorite Fancy Potato Salad

10 Russet potatoes, boiled
1 medium onion, chopped
3 stalks celery, chopped
2 medium pickles, chopped
1 cup mayonnaise
1 cup sour cream
1 tsp. salt (or to taste)
½ tsp. celery salt
¼ tsp. garlic powder
¼ tsp. pepper
½ tsp. dried dill
Tomato (optional for garnish)

Cool potatoes. Remove jackets. Cube. Add remaining ingredients (except tomato) and mix. Taste and adjust seasoning, mayo, and sour cream to your preference for flavor and creaminess. Chill before serving. Garnish with tomato wedges.

NOTE: To make this potato salad vegan, replace mayo and sour cream with soy "sour cream."

Memorial Day

The last Monday in May is currently observed as Memorial Day, set aside to remember those who lost their lives in service to our country. The tradition began with women who laid wreaths on the graves of soldiers lost in the Civil War. Today, veterans of American wars customarily remember the fallen by selling red poppies.

Remembering Loved Ones

We look forward to celebrating a long, fun-filled three-day weekend. Let's party! Bring on the Indiana 500 sports car race, backyard barbecues, and maybe a trip to the beach or amusement park! With the approach of summer, focus is on family fun playing beach or pool games, relieved by hot dogs and hamburgers, chips, and quenching lemonade.

However, for some of us the loss of a loved one to war is painfully immediate. Almost every family has at least one member who has served in the military. This is the time to say thank you to them and their families who have sacrificed so much. It's time for visiting the cemetery, pulling out photos of relatives in uniform, and remembering their lives before the war, their dreams cut short, and their heroic service.

At our parties, we stop to remember their bravery, our communal loss, and their unspeakable contribution to our national cause. We say, "Thank you!" and toast to the memory of their precious lives.

Make-ahead Meal

Food prepared the day before your party allows more time to celebrate the holiday the way you choose. Barbecue a tri-tip beef roast and refrigerate it. When it's cold, it's easier to slice and cut into matchsticks. Cut Jarlsberg Swiss cheese in sticks. Microwave asparagus spears. Slice red onion. Package each of these in plastic bags, including prepared lettuce, grape tomatoes, red onion slices, baby avocados, and lemon wedges to assemble on one huge platter, at the last minute. Or open the bags for

individual salad assembly at a picnic. Bring a bottle of your favorite dressing.

Deviled eggs and watermelon are tasty accompaniments. I included corn fritters with melted butter and syrup for my backyard dinner. Dessert was a homey blackberry and white peach cobbler with vanilla ice cream.

Display *memorabilia.*

Celebrating Heroes

Graduation Celebrations

Graduation celebrations begin in preschool and extend through graduate school! Every one of them is a big deal. Your graduate deserves to be honored for accommodating to a new environment, overcoming trepidations, working hard, learning new skills, accomplishing much, and making new friends.  Graduations mark the early chapters in our lives. Postgraduate course completions deserve recognition, too, especially if it is you, who's earned a pat on the back!

Open House

It has always seemed tricky to me to invite guests to an open house, i.e., a block of time during which they can come and go randomly. However, if you *plan* a "laid back" approach to your production, you can enjoy being with your guests. Such hosting requires either help or putting the "fixings" out for people to mix their own drinks and help themselves to appetizers and desserts on ice or in chafing dishes, while you circulate around the room, welcoming guests and saying your goodbyes.

A Place of Honor

Whether your child is graduating from nursery school, middle school, or high school, there is usually both an individual portrait and a class picture taken at year end. This is a fitting time to display all of these pictures for guests to see.  The latest photo can be the focal point of a table dedicated to and decorated just for the graduate.

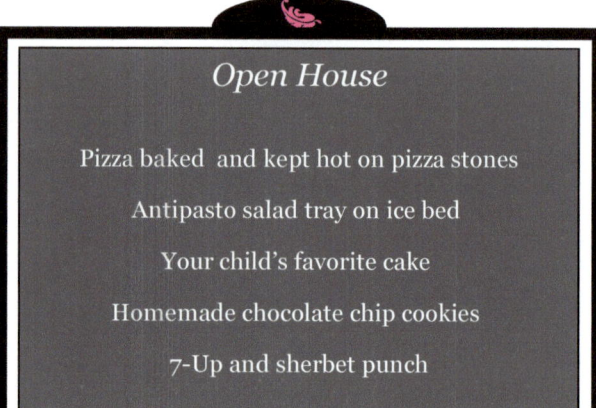

Open House

Pizza baked and kept hot on pizza stones

Antipasto salad tray on ice bed

Your child's favorite cake

Homemade chocolate chip cookies

7-Up and sherbet punch

Use school colors for your refreshment table. Include helium filled balloons, crepe paper streamers, color-coordinated table cloths, napkins, and paper or plastic party ware. These say gaiety, freedom, and fun; whereas, the use of crystal, silver, china, and linen says formality.

Produce a video of still pictures of your graduate to share with family. Add your child's favorite music and graphics; these will enhance the experience for everyone. If you have a video of your child in the actual graduation ceremony at school, play that too!

Honoree Table

1. A photo album of your child.
2. A sport jersey with his or her number.
3. A letterman's jacket.
4. A school report or project your child is fond of.
5. Certificates of achievement.
6. The musical instrument studied.
7. Framed or featured art work created by the artist.
8. Include items that mean the most to your loved one, with his or her permission.

"Staycation"

School's out! Everyone wants to go on vacation, but time and money are in short supply. What to do? People take a "staycation," that's a word invented to mean stay put, to vacation at home or nearby. I've always felt transported by the lure of exotic places depicted in travel posters, some of which are collector's items today. If you have one, pull it out and build a party around it. If you have access to a pool at home or nearby, include swimming fun in your plans, too. My family enjoyed a combined pool and panini party. Panini is Italian for a fancy grilled sandwich, which can include whatever you like, glued together with cheese, on any kind of bread, buttered on the outside.

Try a quick version of *cubanos*, Cuban sandwiches. Opt for roasted pork from the market, thin deli ham slices, swiss cheese slices, and French rolls, plus mustard and pickles. I buttered the top and bottom of the roll and put it into a panini maker, well toward the back, so the lid would close. If you're using a frying pan, try pressing down the sandwich with a bacon press, a foil covered brick, or push hard with a spatula. The idea is to flatten the sandwich as much as possible. When you see the cheese is melting out, you know it's done.

Cuban Cocktails

Set the mood with a Cuba Libre or Dolce de Leche. The former is rum (light or dark), a lime, and cola. I like to use Diet Coke or Diet Cherry Coke, putting the squeezed lime right into a tall glass with plenty of ice. Dolce de Leche means sweetened milk, like sweetened condensed milk (1/2 oz.), which can be combined with rum (1 oz.) and chocolate liquor (1/2 oz.), shaken with ice, then strained into a martini glass or coconut shell! I like to add coconut milk (1/2 oz.), as well. Sarah Brown, in the movie *Guys and Dolls*, drank way too many of these! I recommend that movie or music from it to round out your evening.

Cuba Is Calling

Travel to Cuba from the United States may be possible again for the public. Who can wait? Take a taste trip. Pack some old suitcases, put on a sundress over a swim suit, and blend up some fresh fruit smoothies for lounging by the pool. When hunger strikes, bring out a platter of fixings to make Cuban sandwiches on a panini grill or an electric frying pan outside.

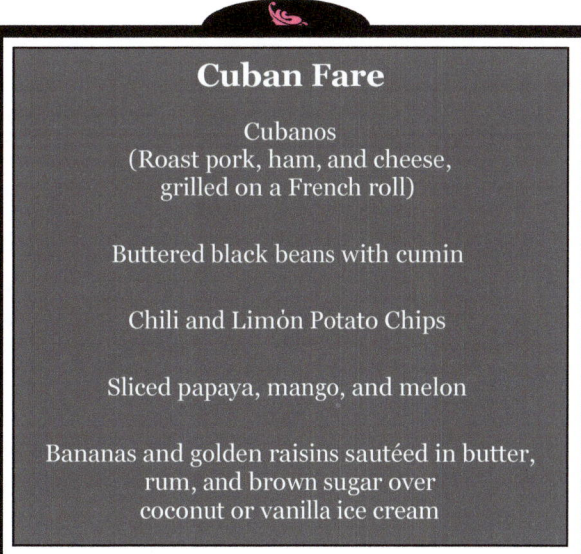

Cuban Fare

Cubanos
(Roast pork, ham, and cheese, grilled on a French roll)

Buttered black beans with cumin

Chili and Limón Potato Chips

Sliced papaya, mango, and melon

Bananas and golden raisins sautéed in butter, rum, and brown sugar over coconut or vanilla ice cream

Father's Day

It's always difficult to find really appropriate Dad's Day cards, it seems. Besides, Dads really appreciate homemade cards even more.

Usually Moms or school teachers put little ones up to the task, but sometimes teens come up with surprises all on their own. Our daughter made a wonderful collage of clippings from magazines for her dad. She cut out pictures that symbolized their times together or her special vision of her dad. She interspersed "sound bites," that is printed

words and phrases. He was deeply touched by this gift. It hangs in his office where he can and does look at it often for inspiration, to be the hero that she sees. She lives on her own now.

Plan Activities

One of the best Father's Days we ever spent with my Dad was when my sisters and I were still pre-teens. He enlisted us in a backyard project—to build a miniature golf course! We had more fun setting up obstacles and cups, pulling out his old clubs, and playing the day away!

My husband loves being challenged to a ping pong play-off with his daughter. My dad used to relish a good family game of horseshoes.

Now, that our daughter is older, she invites her dad out for a game of golf. He loves spending time with her. They have spent many an hour from childhood on, swinging together in the backyard. Pulling together a game of softball or water volleyball (if the pool is warm) are guy ideas of fun.

Camping or Not

If you are lucky to have access to a camper, then a Father's Day weekend outing is a great idea, So long as kids help pull the trip together, so Dad doesn't have to do too much of the work, it can be a real memory-making adventure. Toasting marshmallows over a camp fire to make S'mores is one of life's sweet pleasures.

Kid Coupons

An old favorite are redeemable coupons from kids for: a car wash, lawn mowing, ½ hour of weeding, sweeping out the garage, shoe polishing, head massage, or a box of homemade cookies.

Theme Parties for Dad

1. Godfather (Gangsters and Molls): Roaring 20's attire, red carnations, squirt guns, ginger ale, and gin fizzes.

2. Hero Worship (Dad on Pedestal): togas, "medals of honor" for Dad's great traits, pealed grapes, wine, cheese, turkey drumsticks.

3. Country (Down Home Fun): playing horseshoes, tomatoes planted in overalls, straw hats, buttermilk biscuits, Johnny cakes, and fried chicken.

4. Roots (Ethnic Celebration): clothes, décor, and festivities typical of the "old country" with food the way Grandma made it.

Celebrating Dad

Hearty Food Outdoors

Moms and kids need to take over the barbacue chores for Dad. Plant him in a lounge chair with a tall cool one and some favorite reading material. Make him comfy, encourage him to nap. Tell him you'll wake him when dinner is ready.

Detail dad's car. Stock it with gum, mints, tissues, cool sunglasses, drive-thru gift certificates, map organizer, cup holder, window wipes, and paper hearts. One last touch, a promissory note not to eat in his car.

Barbecue for Dad

Peanuts in the shell
Burgers and hot dogs
or London broil on rye toast
Baked beans
Potato chips or deep-fried onion rings
Cole Slaw
Sliced beefsteak tomatoes
Decadent chocolate cake

George's Black Forest Cake *favorite*

2/3 cup butter
1 2/3 cups sugar
3 eggs
2 ¼ cups flour
2/3 cup cocoa
¼ tsp. baking powder
1 ¼ tsp. baking soda
1 tsp. salt
1 1/3 cups water
1 tsp. vanilla
1 pint cream, whipped
1 can cherry pie filling
Favorite vanilla frosting
Pam with flour

Bake at 350°. Spray 2 layer cake pans. Beat butter, sugar, eggs 5 min. on high. Blend dry ingredients. Add to egg with water and vanilla. Mix on low. Pour into pans. Bake 35 minutes. Cool on rack. Split layers. Cover bottom layer with whipped cream, next with cherries, next with whipped cream. Put last layer on top and frost entire cake. Refrigerate.

Craft a Photo Album

1. Collect photos of Dad from childhood to the present.

2. Group photos chronologically, by certain interests or traits, with the family, or just "the man" at different ages.

3. Insert photos into a 3 ring photo binder.

4. Print out and glue humorous comments or "factoids," using different computer fonts, on each page.

5. Ask your children to draw a picture of their dad to include in the album with a message.

6. Make time on Father's Day for Dad and kids to sit down together to go through the album.

Summer Fun

Summer is all about fun outdoors. June is a great month for morning and evening meals outside. After school ends, outings to the beach, picnics, fishing, hiking, biking, "garage-sailing," and real sailing allow families to share excitement and expend energy!

Bring the Seashore Inside

I keep seashells, collected over the years, in a big box, which comes out right after Father's Day. Lace and a cluster of white "seed berries" evoke sea foam and spray. A crystal decanter with shell stopper suggests light sparkling on water. Setting up such a display is an art form called ornamentation.

Create your own still life!

Garden Party

Time Out

Everybody needs a "time out" once in a while. Children have the luxury of time off from school to "recreate" themselves during summer. Adults definitely need a time out too, or else they are likely to burn out and get cranky. Really take advantage of weekends and extra days off to enjoy the fruits of your labor, to enjoy being outdoors at home. Plan special meals with family and friends at different times, some morning get-togethers and some afternoon events. Plan a mid-summer night's dream, a twilight soiree (lighter than dinner, more like appetizers, aperitifs, dessert, dancing, and cards).

Have a garden party. Ask everyone to wear white. Put up the badminton set.

On a white tablecloth, serve a big white platter of delectable summer fruit (bite-sized, doused in orange juice), grouped by kind, not mixed together. In the center, put a frosty crystal or silver bowl piled high with sweetened, whipped cream. Pre-scoop and chill vanilla ice cream balls for floats. Stack crustless tea sandwiches under a beautiful, wet white tea-towel for guests to reach under, grabbing whatever kind they can reach, sight unseen.

Hook up an outdoor speaker and play some dreamy music: "Somewhere in Time" (John Barry), "The White Peacock" (Charles Griffes), "Aquarium" (Camille Saint-Saens), and "Mephisto Waltz" No.1 S.514 (Franz Liszt). Put magazines and books out to invite reading and dozing. Turn on *Hello Dolly* to boost the energy level. Who knows, maybe someone will burst into song!

Garden Party

Tea Sandwiches:
Cucumber and cream cheese
Egg salad
Walnut, strawberry and cream cheese
Brie and browned onion

Fruit Patter with Whipped Cream
Peaches and plums
Strawberries, blueberries
Blackberries, raspberries
Kiwi and apricots

Floats:
Root beer, sarsaparilla, or orange soda
Vanilla ice cream balls

Shortbread cookies

Tablecloth Transformations

1. Layer white lace tablecloths over plain white ones for a dressier effect.

2. Cover outdoor furniture, such as a swing or settee or hammock with lace or fringed cotton for a cool, summery, Victorian look.

3. Hang lace tablecloths at a window, draped and gathered at one side to add period drama, without obscuring a pretty view.

4. Drape lace tablecloths on either side of sliding bathtub doors to soften their industrial style.

5. Use a lace or other tablecloth as a coverlet over a bed for vintage appeal.

6. Smaller lace pieces placed over a lampshade look old-fashioned, but be sure to use a low voltage bulb positioned low into the shade.

7. Line good quality white flat sheets and pinch pleat for an elegant window covering that will last many years.

8. Square tablecloths make great toppers.

Summer's Day

Extend Indoor Comforts

4th of July

Independence Day calls for bunting, flags, and a backyard barbecue. If you are lucky enough to live near a small town, you might want to take in a morning parade, complete with floats and the local high school band. Kids will want to attend the local fire-works show in the evening.

Sometimes, I decorate my family room mantel with 4th of July paraphernalia right after Father's Day. It's fun to anticipate the holiday. I like to plant red, white, and blue petunias out front, too, or lobelia, white kalanchoe, and geraniums.

Blue and White China

American ships have been bringing nondescript blue and white china to American hostesses since 1784. Delft and Spode became hugely popular European manufacturers, copying Chinese patterns. 4th of July celebrations seem to be the perfect time to feature these charming collectibles.

Decorate with Children in Mind

Dolls make wonderful decorations to catch the notice of children. The Pierot and Pierette French dolls came from the French July 14 Bastille Day celebration we enjoyed in Paris with our daughter, who was then 6 years old. Very dear friends there made a gift of them to her. Did you know both countries have Statues of Liberty? Vive la France!

Showcasing Fabrics

1. Edge napkins or remnants in red and white gingham ribbon.
2. Cover small pillows on one side with a flag and on the other with navy blue felt.
3. Lace, especially against mahogany, suggests the Colonial period of the American Revolution.

4th of July Barbecue

July 4th Barbecue

Artichokes with hummus or Ranch Dip

Fried or grilled chicken

Grilled asparagus and zucchini

Corn on the cob with melted butter

Pasta salad on lettuce greens

Apple or peach pie á la mode

July 5th Corn Salad
favorite

2 cups cooked corn on the cob

1/2 cup grape or halved cherry tomatoes

1/4 cup sliced ripe (black) olives

1 green onion chopped fine

1 cooked artichoke heart diced

1/4 cup Girard's Champagne Dressing

Slice corn from the cob. Mix all ingredients together in a serving bowl. Chill before serving.

4th of July Pageant

The wonderful thing about dramatic play is giving people the freedom to pretend to their heart's content, without judgment or heavy-handed direction. Watching their spontaneous creativity and how the children work together to produce highly original results is part of the larger, day-long entertainment!

Especially if children are visiting from out of town, it's fun to challenge all the kids to put on a show for the adults, illustrative of the historical occasion.

We hauled the electric piano outdoors and microphones, hung up a red tablecloth for a curtain, and gathered the bits and pieces for making costumes. Although the actual show was brief, it was utterly delightful! Children rally to the challenge, because they're used to producing such theatrics at school.

Pageant Creation

1. Start a costume rack, box, or closet for dramatic play. Include period wigs, hats, jackets, britches, dresses, gowns, fans, gloves, crowns, and capes.

2. Uncle Sam might read from the Declaration of Independence.

3. President Washington might share highlights of his life.

4. The host may lead the audience in "America, America" or "The Star Spangled Banner."

Kids Entertain

More than anything else, children want to do what adults do. They try walking around in Dad's shoes or Mom's high heels. Children play house, play pretend, and play at giving their dollies a tea party. Giving them opportunities to decorate and cook for adults is an even bigger thrill, which they may take quite seriously! While supervision is required around heating elements and knives, let kids do all the work!

"Instant" Playhouse

Turn a major appliance box into an instant playhouse. Paint it white, cut a door and a hole for a drop down shelf, held in place with bungee cords. Young children can have so much fun playing in one.

One week, it can be a U.S. Post Office; the next, a super market; the next a gingerbread house with paper bag cookie cut-outs; and then a Bugs Bunny's Bakery! Furnish each "place of business" with appropriate props from around the house.

Birthday Cake Decoration

Allow elementary school age children to decorate their own birthday cake for a party with friends. Think how proud they would be to show-off their creation. Give them food coloring to mix their own frosting. No "just fixing it" here or there or directing their hands! Kid cake decorating is just as charming as kid created art. Be sure to take photos and make over their originality.

Allow *your youngsters to make cookies from scratch...without a recipe. Treat this as a junior science experiment. Let them use any food ingredients you have on hand to see what will happen. No clues. You may be amazed at the results!*

Asian Dinner

Middle school kids are ready to put on a dinner for the family. An easy meal that's pretty fool-proof is a stir-fry. Have all the vegetables sliced and mounded separately from sliced beef or chicken. Heat oil and salt in an electric wok at 375°. Add and cook the meat, then the vegetables that take the longest first, pushing each ingredient up the side of the pan, before adding the next. Finally, stir it altogether and add the sauce. Serve over steamed rice, easily made in a rice cooker.

High school kids can make sushi as an appetizer for this stir-fry meal. Provide the proper utensils and have them prepare the ingredients and sticky rice and make a roll. Praise their work! Sushi chefs apprentice for 10 years!

Midsummer Romance

After Memorial Day through the summer, many cultural and church groups invite the public to enjoy ethnic festivals, which double as fundraisers. Greek festivals are especially known for encouraging novices to join in their lively dances, sample their rich foods, and buy wares procured from the old country. If you are particularly fond of certain cultures and cuisines, share that love with your family and friends. Or, explore new lands through cookbooks. India always calls to me!

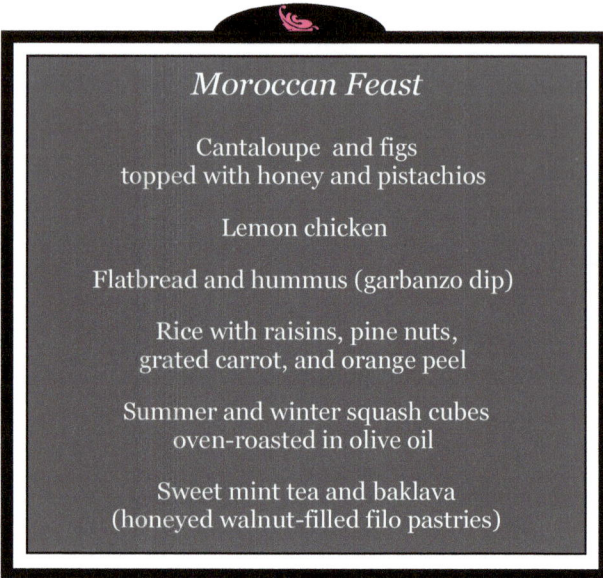

Moroccan Feast

Cantaloupe and figs
topped with honey and pistachios

Lemon chicken

Flatbread and hummus (garbanzo dip)

Rice with raisins, pine nuts,
grated carrot, and orange peel

Summer and winter squash cubes
oven-roasted in olive oil

Sweet mint tea and baklava
(honeyed walnut-filled filo pastries)

Chair a cultural event! You'll probably be asked to do so every year thereafter! Such fêtes are great fun and real money-makers. Otherwise, put on an exotic evening for guests. Create cultural ambiance with music, food, decorations, entertainment, and activities.

At Home Event

Do you have a favorite pastime that revolves around an ethnic theme? Friends talked me into taking a belly-dancing class with them! At the end of it, we had a celebratory dinner Moroccan style. We made belly-dancing costumes and talked our husbands into wearing Middle Eastern garb. We ladies provided the entertainment after dinner, complete with zills (finger cymbals) and veils!

Morocco under the Stars

A long dinner evening of dramatic play can begin outdoors and end inside. We began the evening with appetizers and a dip in the pool, then moved to the kitchen for our meal and entertainment. Moving guests from room to room keeps a party interesting.

To set the stage we hung a billowy Indian bedspread from the four corners of the ceiling and fastened it to the fan (hiding it) in the center. We felt like we were inside a tent. With all furniture removed, the floors were covered with overlapping oriental rugs. A mass of pillows were propped up against the bay window and on the floor for seating around a very large, oval brass platter from which we ate our meal with our fingers, using flatbread to scoop up the lemon chicken and vegetables ringed around a massive mound of rice in the center.

The gentlemen were left to chat, while we ladies changed into our costumes. We danced our way back into our "Casbah" to Arabic music. Dessert and tea followed. It was an evening to remember and laugh over for years to come.

Card Readings

Ever put a quarter into the fortune teller's box at the state fair? Esmeralda would return your fortune on a little card, hopefully announcing that you would be lucky in love or be coming into a vast sum of money!

Most everyone enjoys having their fortunes told, either from a fortune cookie, tarot cards read by a psychic, hands read by a palm reader, or birthdates interpreted by a numerologist or astrologist. Tarot readings can be geared for youngsters through oldsters. They are a popular attraction at fund-raising events and grad night celebrations. They fit surprisingly well into many kinds of parties, especially ethnic gatherings, Christmas and New Year's Eve parties, and Halloween parties. Finishing a romantic Moroccan evening with a round of private, professional readings for guests (who would like to participate) is a very special treat. But, no one should be pressured who prefers not to join in.

Set the Stage

Provide a private corner with low lighting. Hang a tablecloth, bedspread, or beaded curtain over the doorway to create drama. Add ethnic or theme furnishings, accessories, and soft music to enhance an air of mystery. Candles are good, crystal balls, exotic scarves, even a Crazy Eight Ball, if you have one! Set a small table between 2 or 3 chairs. Some guests may want their spouse to sit in. But the reader should protect the seeker's privacy and promise not to share anything that is said with anyone else but the seeker.

Novice Readings

Can't afford a psychic? Learn to be a reader using the "Voyager" deck. The symbols come from *The National Geographic* and evoke feelings just by looking at them. Ask your seeker if he or she has a question for the Universe. Shuffle the deck, fan the cards face down, and have the seeker pick 3 cards: past, present, and future. What do the cards say relative to the seeker's question? As a reader, trust your intuition!

Create Outdoors

No matter what size plot of earth you have to work with, even if it's only dirt in a pot, make the most of it! Use your imagination! My husband's motto is, "From Possibility to Reality." Often the most stubborn problem areas in a yard are calling out for a burst of breakthrough creativity.

What you hated can become what you love the most! Focal points, paths, and destinations can turn a boring yard into a secret garden. A garden window, kitchen counter, or table by a sunny window can be transformed into a wonderland with a small fountain, moss, and colorful annuals tucked into a large basket. An acre of land can be home to fruit trees, a pond, a swing, a vegetable garden, a gazebo, a sculpture garden, maybe even a bocce court!

Take on *a big project as a family. Find plans online or at a "Do-it Center" for an old-fashioned wooden glider or gazebo. Involve everyone in gathering the materials and spending the time to build it. Your family will treasure their experience and creation all the more for having worked together.*

Create Garden Magic

1. If grass won't grow under your big shade tree, put down flag stones and potted ferns to create a private retreat.

2. Outline stars, moons, and ringed planets

   on a large rock, then use blue acrylic paint to fill in around the celestial shapes. Make the rock a prominent feature in your garden. When people ask about it, tell them, "It's heaven on earth!"

3. Create a nautical theme, especially around a swimming pool, with the addition of a pelican sculpture. Affix a life-preserver and/or ship's steering wheel to your pool equipment gate.

4. Add an old-fashioned street lamp to your garden, instead of sidewalk lights, to create a European feel.

5. Build a raised playhouse for the children with a surrounding deck and storage underneath.

Build a Playhouse

Indian Dining

India evokes images of spiritual quests, bathers in the Ganges, blazing saris dipped in gold, lounging Brahma bulls, fragrant spices, and romance á la Taj Mahal. Elephants, Bengal tigers, tropical splendor, incense, sitar music, both incredible poverty and amazing technological progress, and a huge "Bollywood" obsession with movie-making! India is all of this and so much more. Indian cuisine is likewise truly original and complex. It may take living with an Indian roommate to really get the feel for how to cook Indian-style. It's exotic and fascinating. There's much to learn and appreciate, especially in terms of the regional differences of this ancient, multi-faceted culture.

Indian Ambiance

What items do you have around your home which could be pulled together to create an exotic air? Gauzy fabrics in bright colors work and also fringed scarves in solid colors and stripes. Gold, brass, silver, jewels, beads, bangles, tassels, tenting, and turbans all lend that touch of Indian character. Import stores offer many beautiful hanging glass lamps to hold candles, some that look like perforated, three-dimensional stars, which cast dots of light about the room.

Friends have brought back Indian souvenirs for us that we enjoy all year, but especially when we put on an Indian dinner party. One of these is a little dancing puppet in pantaloons, playing his bagpipe. We were also given a pair of carved, velvet-lined boxes, which looks almost like ivory. We were surprised to learn they were made of camel bones!

Condiment Heaven

Indian meals can be as simple as a flatbread or as lavish as a twenty dish buffet, but they always seem to be accompanied by one or more intensely flavored chutneys that kick up the dish several notches! Be sure to include one or more chutneys in your menu. A little goes a long way, though. Even seemingly cool sounding mint chutney can range from piquant to call-the-fire-department hot! When buying prepared chutneys in a jar, check the label for chili content. If you make your own, start mild, for your guests' sake. Other toppers include toasted fresh coconut, cashews, almonds, pistachios, raisins, date syrup, and pomegranate seeds. A cool yogurt concoction is usually also offered to counter the heat of chilies, peppery spices, and ginger.

Daily Naan

If you don't mind having guests with you in the kitchen, put them to work "making their daily bread." Make any of the simple dough recipes ahead of time. Allow them to rest, and then divide them into little balls. Have guests roll out their own bread and stuff it, if they like, with cooked spinach or cauliflower, then roll it out again and fry it. Everyone gets into the act. After frying his bread, the guest can move on to the buffet, to load up his plate. This also gives guests something to do, while each person takes his time selecting dishes and condiments. The process can be repeated for seconds!

Outline *the contours of the Taj Mahal onto a poster board with a marker to make a striking backdrop for your serving table. Use it as is or cut around it.*

Spice Land

The lure of the Spice Islands called to Christopher Columbus back in 1642! India certainly knows how to use spices, but I believe the rest of the world is still trying to catch up. Experts know how to blend and balance spices for use with vegetables vs. meats vs. legumes vs. grains. Northern regions like their blends hot. Take the lead from Chris, search out authentic spice blends in your local Indian market. But before you set sail, first read an Indian cookbook or about Indian cooking online. You'll need that map to help you navigate through the vast array of products available on market shelves.

At first you may feel lost. Having checked your recipes, you'll end up where you want to be at the end of your shopping adventure, enjoying the treasures you brought home.

To Blend or Not to Blend

What we Westerners think of as curry powder is not really a spice, but a blend of spices. Each Indian cook probably has her own unique curry and masala blends, which might even vary each time she makes them.

Rather than buy spice blends at the Indian market, buy the basic, constituent spices that you can also use separately for other cuisines. If your spice cabinet is pretty bare or you're not feeling adventurous, however, go with the curry powder Westerners know in the regular supermarket! Do as the Indians do, heat spices in a frying pan before flavoring food.

Indian Sampler

Pulao - rice with raisins and nuts

Chicken tandoori – in yogurt, grilled

Samosas – deep fried, potato and pea stuffed pastries

Pudla – curried vegetable pancake

Wada – dhal fritters

Sang Pararatha – spinach "tortillas"

Chutneys – date & lemon, mint, coriander, coconut, Major Grey

Raitas – cilantro, cucumber in yogurt

Tuscan melons and oranges

Indian Culinary Terms

1. Masala – cardamom, cumin, cloves, black pepper.
2. Curry – turmeric, paprika, fenugreek, coriander, red and black pepper, cumin, ginger, celery seed, cloves, caraway.
3. Chutney – also known as pickle is made from a wide array of fruits, e.g., mango, mint, coconut, date, apple, plum, and tamarind. A famous old stand-by, my favorite, is Major Grey's Chutney, which is mango based.
4. Raita – yogurt combined with cucumber and mint or other vegetables.
5. Pulse – a large variety of peas and beans, also known as legumes or dhal, daal, dal.
6. Daggery – molasses-based brown sugar, considered especially healthy.
7. Asafoetida (hing) – a powder added to beans to reduce flatulence.
8. Ghee – butter oil rendered out from the milk solids.

Labor Day

This holiday has always dredged up mixed feelings for people. For children and teachers, it means back to school. Ugh! For people who work, it's nice to have a long weekend, but really, "How about a trip to Hawaii instead!" Children and teachers might agree with that sentiment!

Think Summer Fling

Three days is hardly enough time to visit the Hawaiian Islands. Create your own tropical paradise at home. Transform your backyard into a South Seas paradise. Invite guests for a luau, mainland style. Ask them to wear something tropical for the occasion.

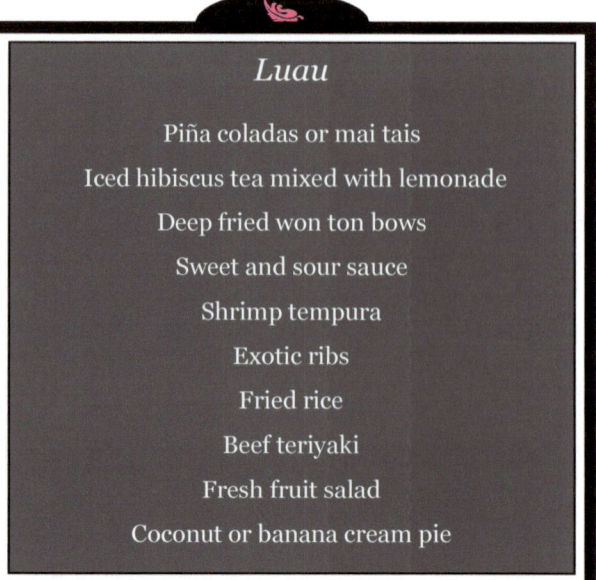

Luau

Piña coladas or mai tais
Iced hibiscus tea mixed with lemonade
Deep fried won ton bows
Sweet and sour sauce
Shrimp tempura
Exotic ribs
Fried rice
Beef teriyaki
Fresh fruit salad
Coconut or banana cream pie

Easy Exotic Ribs
favorite

4 lbs. baby back pork ribs
1/2 cup ketchup or favorite BBQ sauce
1/2 cup hoisin sauce
1/2 cup black bean and garlic sauce
1/2 cup orange marmalade or
apricot jam

Mix sauces (available in Oriental aisle of market) in plastic bag. Cut ribs into 6 sections and toss to coat in bag. Chill for 2 to 6 hours. Place ribs on cake cooling rack on top of foil lined cookie tray. Bake at 350° for 45 min., turn ribs over, and bake for 45 min. more. Cut ribs apart to serve. Offer hot, wet towels after.

Sirius Pops on Satellite Radio has a station that plays Hawaiian music all day. Or, pull out favorite island tapes or CDs. Pull out the ukulele and leis. Rent the musical, *South Pacific*, for a romantic trip to the islands.

Hawaiian Islands Backyard

Seashore Get-Away

Walking, relaxing, and dining by the water are ultimate summer pastimes for families, but especially for couples celebrating a wedding anniversary. If you cannot get away to the ocean, a lake or river, pond or pool, walk to the market for some fresh seafood, instead. Take a refreshing bath or shower, put on something white and flowing, and retire with your best friend to a dinner for two.

Blue Plate Special

Dine *al fresco* (outside) or set up an intimate  table in an unexpected part of the house, where you can throw open the windows and turn on a fan. Gather symbols of the seashore you may have collected, a painting of the beach, blue and white china, fresh flowers, and white linens. Use the good crystal. Provide romantic lighting and music. Have a romantic comedy ready, if the evening is long enough, such as: the foreign film, *Bread and Tulips*; *French Kiss*; or the oldie, *Shirley Valentine*.

The seafood possibilities are endless! My favorite shrimp dish is garlicky, buttery scampi with plenty of lemon and capers. For two, scampi, a summer squash medley, and crusty bread with a salad are enough. To  extend the meal for family, serve the shrimp over linguine with parmesan shreds. Steamed Alaskan king crab legs and lobster, seasoned with Old Bay spice rub, plucked from their shells and dipped in lemon butter are an extravagantly delicious treat for two. For the family, clam chowder with oyster crackers and crab cakes go farther and taste wonderful, as well.

Go fishing with your children. It's an exciting experience kids will remember all their lives.

Another favorite is crab or shrimp Louie salad. The Brown Derby in Beverly Hills used to serve a combination of the two mounded on shredded iceberg lettuce with grated hard-boiled eggs and Louie dressing in a silver boat. You can make your own dressing of ketchup, sweet pickle relish, mayonnaise,  with a dash of lemon juice, and hot sauce. Garnish with Haas avocado slices, lemon wedges, and tomato. Served in a large shell, it looks spectacular!

Bateaux Mouches

The most exciting family excursion we experienced was a two hour dinner cruise, *Bateaux Mouches*, on the River Seine in Paris at sunset. To be honest, I cannot remember what we had to eat, though it was excellent and was accompanied by fresh baguettes, one per person! The city's beauty was so breathtaking and our French hosts so warm and charming. That is what I remember most. As we advanced, the lights blinked on along the riverbanks and over the bridges, causing dancing ribbons to shimmer across the water.

How can you add that kind of glamour to your patio or dining set-up? One way is to string soft outdoor light bulbs over your table or under a patio umbrella and hang a riot of shiny ribbons! Put a bottle of champagne in an ice bucket on the table. Dress up. Play "La Vie en Rose" and zippy accordion music from *French Kiss*. There's nothing like music to instantly transport people to another place and time. Especially if you are housebound or penny-pinching, travel videos can take you to the great rivers of the world. Beautiful travel books are very reasonably priced at a library's used book sale nook. Placed around a room, they can take you or a youngster to an exotic destination within a few minutes and excite dreams that may be realized in a lifetime.

Form a Gourmet Dinner Club

1. Invite 3 other couples to join.

2. Have a dinner party every 2 months, from 6 p.m. to midnight.

3. Hosts publish an international menu and decorate accordingly.

4. Hosts make the main dish and send out recipes to the other couples to bring the appetizers, sides, dessert, and wine. The expense is dispersed that way.

5. All dress the part. Play ethnic music.

6. Even if you cycle through the four couples only once, it's worth it.

Supper on the Seine

Coquilles St. Jacques

Baked whole red snapper

with spinach stuffing

Braised lettuce and leeks

Cherry tomatoes roasted in olive oil

French baguettes

Poached peaches with raspberry puree and crumbled macaroons

Coquilles St. Jacques

favorite

1 ½ cups chicken stock
1 ½ cups dry white wine
3 shallots sliced thin
3 celery stalks with leaves chopped
¼ tsp. white pepper
2 lb. scallops in ½" slices
¾ lb. fresh mushrooms sliced
4 tblsp. butter
5 tblsp. flour
¾ cup milk
2 egg yolks
½ cup heavy cream
1 tsp. salt
¼ cup grated Swiss cheese
white pepper, lemon juice
prepared whipped potatoes

Bring first 5 ingredients to boil. Simmer 20 min. Strain into skillet. Add scallops and mushrooms, cover. Simmer 5 min. Transfer scallops and mushrooms to large bowl. Reduce stock to 1 cup. In pan make butter and flour roux. Whisk in stock and milk. Heat until it comes to a boil. Simmer for 1 min. Mix egg yolks and cream in bowl, keep adding and stirring stock to yolks, 2 tblsp. at a time. Then, whisk egg mixture into stock mixture. Bring to boil and add remaining ingredients except potatoes and cheese. Spoon into buttered shells. Pipe whipped potatoes around outside. Sprinkle cheese over sauce. Bake at 375° in top of oven 15 min. Serve at once.

Autumn Displays

Signs of fall begin in summer. A few oak leaves begin to dot the yard, then a few more. Indian summer seems like a fitting description for that lovely bridge between calendar seasons. However, harvesting actually begins in spring!

Prepare in Spring

It's fun to plan ahead for the special beauty and bounty of fall. My white lilacs bloom very early. I cut half for vases and gifts. The other half is tied with rubber bands and hung upside down from a shelf above my pantry. I do the same with branches from my pink Hawthorne bushes that bloom later.

Lavender is bundled and dried in the same way. My miniature rose bushes actually seem to fill out more for my cutting tiny pink roses to dry. I also keep baby's breath and statice from market bouquets to fill in arrangements.

This year, my bromeliads produced three bracts that dried on the plant! I harvested these before they turned brown to retain their color. By summer's end, my privet hedge produced large clusters of dark purple berries that dried surprisingly well. Find showy flowers to dry, like the proteus, at farmers' markets. Ask about others to dry.

Composing Displays

How would you compose your display? I've grouped dark green eucalyptus with red olive clusters and peacock feathers in a classic vase. Building up from a silver vase, a silver tray holds a green cut-glass bowl full of woodsy scented pot pourri and photos of my husband and me, as kids.

This floral display is rounded out with a green-bordered book, *Aesop for Children*, and a shiny green, reflective porcelain melon.

Bay Window Vignette

Autumn Indoors

Time for a Change

Even after living in our home for nearly twenty years, I find there are still new ways to rearrange the living room furniture! Do you ever get the urge to rearrange? If my husband chances to come downstairs from his office when I'm in mid-move, he quickly does an about face and hides back in his office! It's a girl thing, maybe a nesting instinct, but more likely a desperate need to change something she has control over, when she can control nothing else in her life at the time! Men who meddle in such efforts do so at their own risk!

His and Her Desks

Finding a lovely drop-leaf table at a good price was the inspiration for flanking either side of the fireplace with a reading nook. Look closely. Under each table, a trunk is hiding.

On his table, *101 Golf Courses* is open on top of *New Yorker* cartoons. The basket holds "coffee table" books, e.g., a *New York Tour Guide* and *Tesla*.

On her side, an art book is open to a masterpiece. Also, within easy reach, are favorite history books to peruse by the fire on a chilly October evening.

Traditional Fall Décor

On my morning walks, I pick up pine cones that have dropped onto the sidewalk. They fill in a basket nicely with gourds. But, pumpkins say Fall more than any other symbol. If your space for decorating is limited, choose a pumpkin, even a small, solitary one to acknowledge the season's change. It will remind you that time has not passed without your noticing.

***Fill** a basket or punch bowl full of pomegranates and grape clusters, faux and/ or real, to create a dramatic centerpiece for a family dinner.*

Conversational Grouping

Halloween Festivities

Everyone can get into the act at Halloween. My husband traditionally dons his Dracula costume to answer the door for trick-or-treaters. He really gets into character.

For little visitors, he becomes The Count from Sesame Street, "How do I love your costume? Let me count the ways!" I was his assistant for his best performance. I would suddenly open the front door when he was in position upside down on his "gravity inversion" devise, cocooned in his cape. When the door was opened, he would fling his arms out, revealing the cape's red satin lining like giant bat wings. It was a jaw-dropping event that kids and parents clamored for each year thereafter!

Party Ideas

Elementary school children like short games and activities. My experience has been with girls. I'm not sure how active activities need to be for boys! If you dare have a Halloween party for middle school kids, be sure to have plenty of authoritative supervision, with well-planned activities. Left to their own devices, this age group's idea of partying can quickly get out of control!

A large black plastic cauldron can hold an orange soda and orange sherbet punch or cider with clove-studded oranges. Cake doughnuts with black or orange frosting and sprinkles are always a big hit. After party games, if there's time or a sleepover involved, offer a favorite movie: *Nightmare Before Christmas* or *Abbot and Costello Meet Frankenstein*.

Decorations

My parties do not include faux (or real) body parts, rats, lizards, or snakes (unless the latter are of the gummy candy variety)! Paper honey-comb spiders and bats made from black construction paper are welcome and used liberally. Thick black yarn strung from the ceiling of a party room across a corner to the adjacent walls makes a fine spider web, the bigger, the better. To make a goblin, place a witch or wizard hat on a pumpkin head, sitting atop a cloth covered snack tray. Fasten white sheets around helium-filled balloons to hang in doorways as ghosts. Jack-o-lantern lights strung across the front window or fireplace or bannister, with low room lighting give an eery glow. Creepy music and sounds, dry ice coming out of a cauldron, and unexpected ghouls made from clothes stuffed with newspaper, topped with masks and wigs are spooky additions. Display pumpkins your family has carved.

Halloween Entertainment

1. Play pass the orange under one's chin (no hands allowed).
2. Bob for apples or better yet, first one to take a bite out of a hanging apple wins (no hands allowed).
3. Kids swirl and decorate their own caramel apples to take home.
4. Kids take photos of each other making scary or funny faces.
5. They dance and sing on stage with a microphone to popular music.
6. Play limbo under the witch's broom.

Pumpkin Carving Party

Orange pumpkins, green pumpkins, white pumpkins. Several-hundred-pound giants down to palm-size cutie-pies. Their variety and availability invite creative play and display. Children love to carve pumpkins, especially older kids. But, why relegate all the fun just to the younger set? Pumpkin carving has become a more specialized art over time. Challenge the men in your family to come up with their own unique pumpkin designs. Give them plenty of room, lots of supplies and tools for cutting and scraping and scooping, and a little tutorial on techniques. No prizes for first place, though. This is not about competition. It's about creative license and FUN!

Creative Milieu

Incentives are encouraged, however. Promise them the reward of a hearty meal, when they finish! Creativity is spurred by music. Play something to get them into an energetic, creative mood. Spooky is good. Music from *Phantom of the Opera* should do the trick. Insert candles into their completed works. Make them the centerpieces of your dining table. Adjust the room for mood lighting to show off and admire their work!

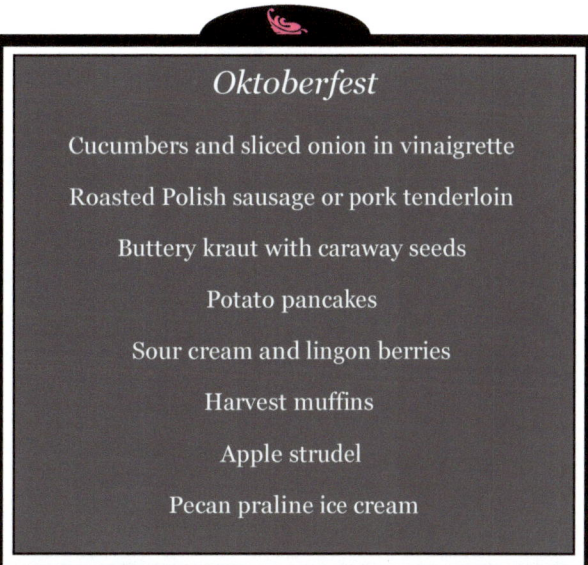

Oktoberfest

Cucumbers and sliced onion in vinaigrette

Roasted Polish sausage or pork tenderloin

Buttery kraut with caraway seeds

Potato pancakes

Sour cream and lingon berries

Harvest muffins

Apple strudel

Pecan praline ice cream

Pumpkin Carving Techniques

1. Draw designs on the pumpkin with indelible markers.
2. Paint designs with bright acrylics.
3. Cut out holes in triangular, circular, diamond, or free form shapes.
4. Plug carved holes with gourds or vegetables (carrots, beets, parsnips)
5. Draw features, then scrape away pumpkin skin to expose features 3-dimensionally.
6. The more flesh carved away in patterns, the brighter the glow.
7. Sculpt and combine more than one pumpkin.

Caution! Carved pumpkins last for a day or two, before they sprout moldy hair!

Harvest Muffins
favorite

2 cups flour

¾ cup sugar

2 tsp. cinnamon

2 tsp. baking soda

½ tsp. salt

4 oz. applesauce (snack cup)

¾ cup canola oil

½ cup undrained crushed pineapple

2 cups grated carrots

½ cup chopped pecans or walnuts

½ cup golden raisins

½ cup coconut

Preheat oven to 350°. Combine dry ingredients. Combine applesauce, oil, and pineapple. Stir into flour mixture. Fold in rest of ingredients. Fill greased muffin pans (makes 15). Bake 30 min. Vegan friendly.

Halloween

Let the little kid in you come out to play! If you are planning a party, you must decorate indoors! But, even if you are only passing out candy, take the time to stage an All Hallow's Eve wonderland at your door.

The Old Oak Tree

A beautiful 130 to 180 year old oak tree stands on the knoll (and lot line) between our house and the neighbors'. They can reach a perfect branch on their side from which to hang and eerily light a gossamer ghost. Beneath it, they surprised everyone with a blow up death coach, driven by a skeleton, drawn by a donkey! The coach lanterns were lit and scary sounds emanated! Ooo-eee!

Favorite Witch and Ghoul

Oddly enough, our little metal witchy-poo came by way of my husband's hospital visit for an appendectomy! It was a get-well gift from my sister and parents! She takes center-stage inside before Halloween, then meets trick-or-treaters at the door.

Trade *out floral patio cushions for black furry ones. Combine funny, cute décor with scary elements to keep the effect light for little children! Have a Halloween tablecloth too ghastly to grace your table inside? Fold it around a cushion on your patio.*

Trick or Treat

Gobblin' Good Sweet Potato
favorite

4 medium sweet potatoes scrubbed

8 pitted ripe black olives

1 can S&W Caribbean black beans

1 cup tomato salsa

1 cup Ranch Dip (sour cream + mix)

1 lime cut into quarters

1 bag nacho or blue tortilla chips

Bake potatoes at 350º 1 hr. until soft. Fill olives with sweet potato. Heat beans, spoon into split potatoes. Dollop 1/4 cup dip on beans. Ring dip with salsa. Place olive eyes upright. Place lime smile on dollop face. Serve with tortilla chips.

Veteran's Day

Veteran's Day falls on November 11 and is especially commemorated with the President placing a wreath at 3 p.m. on the Tomb of the Unknown Soldier. This solemn day is observed in Europe, too, remembering all who have fought in wars. This holiday was originally called Armistice Day, commemorating the end of World War I on 11/11/18. That was supposed to be "The War to End All Wars." It was later changed to Veteran's Day to honor veterans of all wars.

Remember Old Soldiers and New

Children can be asked to make thank you cards, decorated with flags, hearts, and flowers for the vets in the family. It's time for pulling out photos of relatives in uniform.

Family Picnic

As fall approaches, Veteran's Day is the perfect time to organize a hike or touch football in the park. Load up a picnic basket with hot soup, crusty bread, cheese, sparkling grape juice, and cupcakes or cookies with red, white, and blue sprinkles. Sometimes it is quite painful for vets to talk about their war experiences. But, if they choose to do so, counsel children to listen respectfully. Likewise, their questions need to be honored, too.

Call out your beloved vets' names and say, *"Wish you were here!"*

favorite Navy Bean Soup

1 bag dried navy beans
3 smoked ham hocks
2 tbsp. olive oil
1 large onion chopped
2 cloves garlic chopped
2 carrots chopped
3 stalks celery chopped
1 ½ quarts chicken stock
2 tsp. salt (or to taste)
1 tsp. dried marjoram
1 tsp. dried thyme
1 tsp. dried parsley
½ tsp. powdered savory
chopped onions and shredded cheddar

Soak beans in water overnight. Sauté vegetables in oil. Add drained beans, ham, spices, and stock. Bring to boil. Simmer for 1 ½ hrs. Remove hocks, trim off meat and return to pot. Serve topped with raw onion and cheese.

Creating a Tribute

1. Make a place at home or create a box to take on your outing.

2. Put in photos of all your family vets.

3. Decorate the setting or box with red, white, and blue paper, streamers, flags, and gold and silver stars.

4. Include thank you cards & love notes.

5. Include a candle to light, invoking the loved one's spirit to join the party.

6. Say thank you and offer a prayer for an end to all wars and the suffering they cause.

Tapas Party

I first enjoyed tapas in a cozy restaurant on a blustery day in Canada! Indigenous to Spain, tapas are appetizers, served with wine, fine sherry, or cider. It's said that during the Middle Ages, King Alfonso was served a glass of wine with a piece of ham or bread on top of it. Hence, the name tapa, meaning cover or lid. He so enjoyed the combination that he decreed that henceforward, wine should always be served with a little bit of food in tavernas. The objective was to keep workers from getting light-headed from drinking wine without eating, because they could not afford food. Now, tapas are served all over Spain to stave off hunger between early morning and late afternoon meals.

Tapas Bar

A leisurely visit with friends over wine and an array of tapas at home can be as much fun as in a tapas bar. Tapas can be as simple as a bowl of olives

or salted nuts or as fancy as puff pastry empanadas stuffed with spinach, raisins, anchovies, and pine nuts. Typically, new potatoes are steamed or roasted and served with aioli sauce or doused in olive oil favored with Spanish paprika. Meats might include sliced, roasted chorizo sausages or tiny Spanish meatballs in almond or red pepper and tomato sauce. Sundried tomatoes, lemon zest, lemon juice, a bunch of cilantro, and olive oil whirred in a food processor make a delicious sauce to go with deep fried shrimp or little quiches made with Manchego cheese.

Tapas Meal

How many tapas should be served? If you are making a meal of them, then serve six to eight prepared dishes along with crusty peasant bread, olives, and grapes. If you are following the tapas with a main dish, such as a hearty paella of rice, chicken, sausage, and shellfish, then three prepared dishes should be enough. Tapas are so good; they disappear very fast! If any of your guests have been to Spain, invite them to share slides or videos of their trip or get a travel video from the library to play, if guests are inclined to watch it after dinner. Classical Spanish guitar music would be a perfect background to your party or enjoy the symphonic "The Three-Cornered Hat" by Manuel de Falla.

Wine Tasting

In California, grapes are picked to make wine from August through early November, champagne grapes first, before they have sweetened with time. It's exciting to visit a bustling vineyard at harvest. Fairly new to California, we were invited by a friend to come stomp the truckload of grapes he'd brought home to make his own wine in his huge vat. When we arrived at his reclusive home in Topanga Canyon, we were quite shocked to find that the stompers already at work were nude! He had thoughtfully provided a very large hot tub nearby, also made from a tall wine barrel, ...only in California! What would you do in that situation? Jump in?

Fun Wine Tasting

For a company party with 12 to 18 people, 4 to 6 wines should suffice. For a small dinner party, ask each couple to bring 1 bottle of their favorite white or red wine in a paper bag, with price noted inside, tied at the top. Remove the foil from the bottle necks. Remove the corks to let the wine breathe. Number the bags.

Provide preprinted note pads for scoring the wines and describing their appearance, aroma, taste, and aftertaste. Provide each guest with a cup to spit out the wine after tasting it. Drinking too much wine saturates the palette, so that flavor differences cannot be detected. Only 2 oz. or ¼ cup should suffice per person per tasting.

For a larger party, each guest should have a numbered placemat with an array of glasses with the wine already poured. The taster would move from first to last, whites to reds, scoring each wine.

For a smaller, more informal party, you can serve the numbered wines, one at a time for scoring. Then, remove and wash the glasses for the next round, etc. Between rounds, guests cleanse their palettes with bread and sample cheeses.

After all the tasting is completed, compare notes and overall scores for the revealed wines. Sometimes, guests are surprised to find the cheapest wine is the group's favorite!

The tasting can be followed by a flavorful Italian dinner of antipasti, pasta with meat, and a fruity ice.

Italian Dinner Finale

Tasting Steps

As the host, educate those new to wine-tasting. Be the "expert." Demonstrate and explain the 5 part process, marking down notes for each step in the process:

"First, look at the wine. Hold it to the light against a white background. Is the color clear and brilliant? Older wines may have more residue and deeper color. Slosh it around in the glass to see what "legs," or drips it leaves on the glass, as it falls back. Thin trails mean it's a light-bodied wine. Heavier trails equal full-bodied.

Second, smell the wine. Swirl and sniff for first impression. Put nose into glass and take deeper whiff. How would you describe its aroma? Is it intense? Try to detect its body or sweetness.

Third, taste the wine. Take a big sip, enough to fully coat all areas of the tongue. Slosh it about on the tongue. Perse lips to suck in a little air. How would you describe its flavor? Is the taste complex?

Fourth, spit out the wine and notice the aftertaste in your mouth. Is it light, smooth, biting, rich? Is it flavorful? What flavors do you detect?"

Scoring Suggestions

Fifth, give points to each numbered wine:
- 5 = delicious, want more
- 4 = enjoyed it
- 3 = it's good
- 2 = not so good
- 1 = don't like it

Supply *only red wines. Have guests try to guess which numbered wine is the Merlot, Petit Syrah, Cabernet, or Burgundy!*

Multo Bene Mangi

Antipasti
Italian salami with provolone
Baked figs with fontina wrapped in procuitto
Olives and peppers
Coponata (eggplant appetizer)

Pasti
Lasagne or fettucine
with Bolognese and Alfredo sauces
Zucchini in garlic and onion butter
Garlic bread

Italian ice or cannoli (from bakery)

Thanksgiving

Every year there's much to be grateful for. However, putting together Thanksgiving dinner can be such a hectic endeavor, there's no time to be still, to reflect, to enjoy one another's company.

Alternative Celebrations

If it weren't for disappointing everyone expecting a traditional meal, I'd rather pack up a large picnic basket with roasted vegetable and turkey sandwiches, cranberry sauce, chips, and pumpkin brownies to dine under beautiful trees in Peter Strauss National Park. Afterward, we could throw around a Frisbee, take a hike, or sit quietly sipping hot cider from a thermos, remembering, sharing, maybe even singing to a guitar.

Giving to Others

Guilt always sets in, too. Wouldn't it be even more satisfying to help serve dinner to those truly in need? Donating food to Manna; clothes to charities; funds to support micro-loans for impoverished women, children, schools, and mosquito nets; and time with those forgotten in nursing homes — these are just some of the many ways to show gratitude all year through.

Keeping It Simple

One of our best Thanksgiving meals was the simplest. My daughter was two weeks late being born. We didn't want to possibly strand guests or be away from home on Thanksgiving Day, as she was expected at any moment.

Simple Supper

Sliced deli turkey breast
rolled around stove-top stuffing

Turkey gravy from a jar

Homemade mashed potatoes

Cranberry sauce from a can

Store-bought pumpkin pie with Cool Whip

Relax *and don't obsess on doing it all yourself. Some of the best conversations take place while washing the dishes with a friend!*

At Home Entertainment

1. Young at heart guests enjoy charades, board games, cards, or dominoes.

2. If you have an iron skillet, try roasting chestnuts over an open flame. When they pop open, serve them hot in comic newspaper cones, like the Parisians do.

3. Coax the pianists or guitarists in your party to play for a sing-along.

4. Clue: the game is "Black Magic." Guests pick object while accomplice is out. Upon her return, you ask, "Is this object 'it'?" "Yes' for object after the black object queried. Guests try being accomplice.

Thanksgiving Banquet

Food Presentation Tips

1. Push your banquet (dining) table up against a wall that's got eye appeal.

2. Repeat the colors of the wall paintings in your fabric choices. Mix up patterns.

3. Use complementary colors for best effect, such as gold and purple or blue and orange.

4. Place food at different heights. Use baskets and cake plates for elevation.

5. Thanksgiving is about abundance. Display pumpkins, gourds, pomegranates, and grapes.

6. Combine rustic with elegant elements. Use silver casseroles for sparkle.

7. Garnish white dips with fresh herbs, such as cilantro and dill. Fill in platter gaps with flowering kale (more purple) and rosemary.

8. Provide warm lighting for intimate, 5 star restaurant ambiance.

Thanksgiving Choices

Pick and Choose

Appetizers

Butternut squash soup
Cranberry-topped baked brie
with toasted baguette slices
Smoked trout or potted shrimp
Carrots and celery with dip

Side Dishes

Mashed potatoes and gravy
Candied or mashed sweet potatoes
Buttered peas or Brussels sprouts
Green bean, mushroom soup,
and French fried onion casserole
Corn pudding
Turkey and sausage dressing
Wild rice stuffing
Cranberry sauce or relish
Hot rolls and butter

Main Dishes

Whole oven-roasted turkey
Oven-roasted turkey breast
Oven-roasted rolled turkey
Spit-roasted whole turkey
Whole deep-fried turkey
Oven-roasted chicken
Oven-roasted Cornish hens
Roast turkey from the market

Desserts

Pumpkin pie
Pumpkin chiffon pie
Pumpkin cheesecake
Mincemeat pie
Pecan pie
Apple pie
Sweet potato pie

Most people expect traditional fare at Thanksgiving meals. To be safe, pick 1 or more dishes from the menu above. Few people are willing to have Indian curry or Greek pitas or Mexican enchiladas for Thanksgiving, no matter how specially prepared. And, don't try to have prime rib! You might get away with roast pork loin, if that happens to be Grandpa's favorite; but, you'll have to have turkey for everyone else, except for your sister, who's a vegan. However, she might be the only one who'll go for strawberries in balsamic syrup!

Thanksgiving Buffet

Set Up Serving Stations

1. Soup and bread tea-cart

2. Wine bar and cheese side-board or appetizer table with serve yourself beverage bar

3. Dinner buffet with large platter to hold turkey and dressing and covered casseroles for vegetables

4. Dessert table with coffee service

5. Cordial service and chocolates on coffee table

6. Supply of hand towels in the powder room

7. If using paper or plastic service, a designated, lined disposal basket

8. A designated counter or table for used dishes

Afterword

Away We Go!

My husband and I rarely miss a Saturday morning of garage sales. Why shop yard sales and estate sales? Because, the merchandise is often very good quality, difficult to find, and the price is right!

The Universe Provides

My father is of the belief that the Universe will provide. Miraculously, it so often does at garage sales. But, you have to know what you want, and you have to be patient. What would you like to find at a garage sale? Tell the Universe. Then, steadfastly get out there every Saturday morning, so the Universe can offer it to you! Get into the spirit of treasure hunting!

***Play** house. Use your home as an ever-changing canvas for creative self-expression. Please yourself and delight the sensibilities of your family and friends. Whether you have a lot of money or a little, there's always a way. Go ahead. Experiment. Have fun. Have a Goldilocks kind of day—"just right"—all year long.*

Take Another Look

The next time you browse through this book, look for my garage sale finds. Be inspired to hunt for treasure, too. Here's a partial list:

basket full of poinsettias, lamps with marble balls and beaded leather shades, white wicker rocker and stool, white glass-topped wrought iron coffee table, wicker plant stands, kitchen toile curtains, 3-tiered plate stands, green partitioned window mirror, desk top mirror, burgundy leaf plates, velvet Christmas tree skirt, a cut-glass punch bowl, Swedish pyramid with propeller, silver vase, a set of dark blue china, a Tiffany lamp, Chinese fan, green ginger jars, green cocktail glasses, brown pitcher with white flowers, pole lamp with black shade, floral plates, terra cotta casseroles, bed tray, blue depression era glass plates, English picnic basket, Roman plaster bust and pedestal, 1930 white pitcher, wicker lawn furniture, garden fairy, wooden pelican, Tiki masks, black oval floral coffee table, red velvet drapes, brass peacock fire screen, his and her "desks," Halloween door bucket, ghoul, stacked jack-o-lanterns, Halloween tablecloth, and black floral pillows.

Index

A
Adams, John 23
African sampler 18
Amaryllis, 17, 35, 36
Appetizers 11, 71, 74
Asian dinner 49
Autumn 60

B
Badminton 43
Barbecue 41, 47
Baskets 8, 9, 16, 17, 27, 73, 75
Bateau Mouches 59
Blue plate special 58
Book favorites 18, 23, 60
Breads
  Date nut 11
  Easter 31
  Irish Soda Bread, Annie's Famous 25
  Naan 54
  Stollen 11
Breakfast in bed 20, 34
British bangers 12
Brunch 35

C
Cake, George's Black Forest 41
Calla lily 18
Card readings 51
Caribbean food 18
Carver, George Washington 18
Centerpieces 14, 16, 25
Children's activities 9, 15, 16, 40, 48, 49
China, blue and white 46
Chinese New Year 19
Christmas 8, 9, 10, 11, 12, 13
Cinco de Mayo 33
Cocktails 39
Coffee bar 28
Condiments 54
Conversational grouping 63
Coquilles St. Jacques 59
Corn Salad, July 5th 47
Crab Louie 58
Crafts
  Bird cone 16
  Coffee turntable 28
  Fir branches 12
  Honoree table 38
  Painting 19, 27
  Pine cones 13
  Photo album 41
  Pomegranate bowl 62
  Taj Mahal 54
  Tribute 68
  Video 38
Creole food 18
Croquet 21, 43, 44
Cuba 39

D
Danish traditions 12
Decorating
  Birthday cake 49
  Dolls, with 46
  Egg dying 30
  French design 28
  Food, with 17
  Halloween 66
  Outdoor 32
Desks, his and hers 62

E
Easter 30, 31
Eggs 30, 31
Entertainment
  Belly-dancing 50
  Card reading 51
  Chinese New Year 19
  Christmas 11
  Easter 30, 31
  Father's Day 40
  Fishing 58
  Frying bread 54
  Mother's Day 34
  New Year 14
  President's Day 22, 23
  Pumpkin carving 65
  St. Patrick's Day 24
  Tapas party 69
  Thanksgiving 72
  Wine Tasting 70, 71

(Continued on page 79)

Index

F
Father's Day 40, 41
Fiesta 33
Finger food 15
Flags 22, 36, 37, 46, 47, 48
Flowers
    Abutilon 43
    Amaryllis 17, 35, 36
    Bromeliads 43
    Calla lily 18
    Hollyhocks 26
    Hydrangeas 10
    Lavender 60
    Lilacs 26, 60
    Paperwhites 17
    Privet berries 8, 60
    Pussy willows 17
    Roses 15, 37
Food presentation 73
Forced bulbs 17
4th of July 46, 47, 48
Frederick Douglass 18
French food 15

G
Garage sale finds 77
Garden ideas 26, 27, 32, 43, 52, 60
Gift ideas 9, 12, 22, 34, 41
Gourmet dinner club 59
Graduations 38

H
Halloween 64, 65
Harriet Tubman 18
Hawaiian Islands backyard 57

I
Indian culinary terms 55
Indian dining 54, 55

J
Japanese sushi 49

K
King Alfonso 69
King, Coretta Scott 18
King, Martin Luther King 18

L
Labor Day 56
Lace 24, 43, 44
Letter to Santa 9
Linens 26, 27, 43, 46
Lincoln, Abraham 22
Love tokens 21
Luau 56

M
Make-ahead meals 35, 36
Martin Luther King Day 18
McCullough, David 23
Memorial Day 36
Moroccan feast 50
Mother's Day 34, 35
Movie favorites 15, 23, 33, 39, 58, 59
Muffins, Harvest 65
Music favorites 8, 14, 19, 43, 48, 64, 69

N
New Year 14, 15

O
Oktoberfest 65
Open house 38
Outdoor decorating 32, 43, 52

P
Pageant, 4th of July 48
Paninis 39
Paris 28, 29, 59
Parties
    Christmas trimming 8
    Company holiday 11
    Croquet wonderland 21
    Ethnic 24
    Garden 43
    Halloween 64, 65
    Moroccan 50

(Continued on page 80)

Index

    Tapas 69
    Themes for dad 40
    Valentine 21
    Wine tasting 70
Peking Pancakes 19
Picnic 46, 68
Pie, Rachel's Cherry Cream Cheese 23
Play house 6, 77
Playhouse ideas 16, 49, 53

Potato Salad, Fancy 35

President's Day 22
Pumpkins 8, 62, 64, 65, 67
Punch 11, 38
Pussy willows 17

Q
Queen of Hearts 20

R
Red pepper sauce, with tomatoes 69
Ribs, Easy Exotic 56
Rice pudding 12
Robinson, Jackie 18

S
Sandwiches 15, 39, 43
School programs 18, 48
Sculptures 3, 16, 20, 27, 30, 32, 34, 40
Sea shells 42
Seashore 42, 58
Seine, River 59
Serving pieces 29
Serving tables 8, 11, 15, 33, 35, 54, 73, 75
Set design 6, 7, 13, 16, 17, 19, 20, 22, 24, 26, 28, 33,
   36, 42, 47, 51, 60, 61, 66
Soiree, Parisian 29
Soul food 18
Soup, Navy Bean 68
Spa treatment 34
Spice land 55
Spring 26, 27, 28, 60
St. Patrick's Day 24, 25
"Staycation" 39
Summer 42, 43, 44, 56
Sun-dried Tomato Spirals 11
Sweet Potato, Gobblin' Good 67

T
Tablecloths 43
Table settings 12, 14, 19, 22, 23, 25, 35, 38, 74
Tapas party 69
Tasting steps, wine 71
Tea party 21, 43
Terra cotta 33
Thanksgiving 8, 72, 73, 74, 75
Toast, Irish 25
Traditions
    Christmas 12
    Easter 30
Tree
    Decorations 8, 9,
    Oak 66, 76
Tribute, Veteran's 68
Trick or treat 67
Tri-tip salad 36

U
Universe 77

V
Valentine's Day 20, 21
Veteran's Day 68

W
Washington, George 22, 23, 48
Wine tasting 70, 71
Winter 16, 17
Wreaths 26

Y
Yam Bams (biscuits) 23

Z
Zills (cymbals) 50

Kapaka Senko lives in Los Angeles with her husband, George. She loves to "play house," decorating her home for changes in the seasons and holidays. Hosting themed parties at home and in her garden is one of her favorite things to do, prompting her to both research and share new recipes and develop a range of activities to entertain guests.

With a background in literature, project management, and education, Kapaka organizes her suggestions in easy-to-read "bites." Her tips and photos show readers just how to create year round magic at home that both adults and children will enjoy.

www.ingramcontent.com/pod-product-compliance
Lightning Source LLC
Chambersburg PA
CBHW041542220426
43664CB00002B/29